D1237841

A Sociology of Belief

A WILEY-INTERSCIENCE PUBLICATION

JOHN WILEY & SONS
New York • London • Sydney • Toronto

A Sociology of Belief

JAMES T. BORHEK • RICHARD F. CURTIS

Library of Congress Cataloging in Publication Data

Borhek, James T 1930-
A sociology of belief.

"A Wiley-Interscience publication."
Bibliography: p.
Includes index.
1. Belief and doubt. 2. Knowledge, Sociology of.
I. Curtis, Richard F., 1931- joint author.
II. Title.

BD215.B65 301.2'1 74-26584
ISBN 0-471-08895-1

Printed in the United States of America
10 9 8 7 6 5 4 3 2 1

For ABB and MCC

maintain *validation* and *commitment*—the processes in which ideas are made believable and in which they sometimes become unbelievable. Validity and validation are two separate and distinct issues. The explanation for one's belief that the earth is more or less round may be that one was a member of a given grade school class at a given time in a given place. The earth may also, quite independently, be round.[1]

The central problem is not whether ideas are socially conditioned, but how humans come to be so firmly attached to them and how that attachment functions in social organization. That is, we find the problem of belief sociologically more interesting than the problem of knowledge. The very mention of belief calls the sociology of religion to mind, but belief is a *general* social process, and to restrict the study of belief to religious institutions is to miss the point. We take such classics as *Elementary Forms of the Religious Life* to refer most significantly to social life in general rather than to churches or doctrines of the supernatural.

Unlike some contemporary formulations in the sociology of knowledge, this is a *sociology* of belief, not a psychology, social psychology, or phenomenology of belief.[2] With a minimum of exceptions, we maintain a sociologistic frame of reference. This is

[1] The problem of ascertaining validity is one of the two main traditional concerns of sociologists of knowledge and arises as soon as one accepts the premise that no matter how real the world "out there" may be, one perceives it and communicates about it in terms of socially learned concepts and language. This fact, discussed in detail in Mannheim (1936), seems to be the root source of two other arguments in the sociology of knowledge which have generated more heat than light: the problem of relativism, for which see Mannheim (1936) and Taylor (1956); and the "what is ideology" argument, for a summary of which see Harris (1968:1-26) and Geertz (1964). The former argument is not within the domain of this book and is probably a paradox and therefore insoluble. Geertz (1964) dubs it "Mannheim's Paradox." The latter problem we regard as existing largely because of an unwillingness of scholars to admit that all statements about the social bases of knowledge made by social scientists apply to the statements made by the social scientists. See our discussion of the problem of self-reference off and on throughout the book.

The second major concern of the sociology of knowledge (and which obtains to social psychology as well) is the relationship that obtains between mental phenomena and social organization. This is the topic with which this volume is concerned.

[2] That is, to pick three specific examples, our perspective is different from that of Berger and Luckmann (1966), Nettler (1970), and Rokeach (1960, 1968).

not to deny the utility of psychological or phenomenological analyses of belief, belief systems, or believing. It is, rather, an attempt to approach a fascinating empirical and theoretical problem from a purely sociological framework. Thus, rather than focusing on the believer and the social supports for *his* beliefs, we will focus on the things believed, and their relations to social organization. This will be discussed in greater detail in Chapter 3. It is not that the believer is unimportant—simply that this book is not about him.

We will operate within a theoretical framework based on the following five very general propositions:

1. Belief systems are cultural in nature. Belief is an aggregate phenomenon that requires explanation in aggregate terms.

2. Belief systems exist in two social contexts, a context of meaning and a context of social organization; unless both of these contexts are understood, beliefs are not intelligible.

3. The explanation for the persistence of belief systems is that people become and remain committed to them, but for commitment to persist the belief system must be validated.

4. The explanation for the rise and change of belief systems lies partly in the fact that they have utility in group adaptation to strain or disorder but also partly in the fact that:

5. Although belief systems are preeminently social facts (as emphasized in the above four propositions), they have nonsocial aspects, such as an internal logic, that drive them in given directions regardless of the wishes of the believers.

This theoretical backbone is basic to the organization of our chapters.

Belief systems are defined in Chapter 1. Their defining properties are discussed in relation to the problems of studying belief, and system parts—the elements of belief—are presented. The problem of definition is continued in Chapter 2, which presents a set of descriptors: variable characteristics according to which belief systems may be classified.

The logical implications of the cultural nature of belief systems (proposition 1) are traced in Chapter 3. The contexts of belief (proposition 2) are examined in Chapter 4, and the social processes that maintain belief through commitment (proposition 3) are presented and discussed in Chapter 5. The tendency of belief systems to lead, through their own inner logics, instead of merely following the interests of believers (proposition 5) appears throughout the whole book, though it is most concentrated in Chapter 6.

Chapter 6 takes up the various ways in which beliefs are supported in their own terms: the process of validation. This is the central problem in the sociology of belief. How is it that congeries of symbols can continue to compel the commitment of humans, specifically through their claims to truth (rather than convenience), when there is good reason for the humans to doubt? Herein lies the power of belief that makes it an independent force in human affairs. Principles of validation free beliefs from simple subservience to collective interests, and commitment yields the means by which humans are affected.

This theoretical orientation is applied to a specific societal context, urban society, in Chapters 7 and 8. Thus Chapter 7 attempts to show what it is about urban social conditions that makes the kinds of beliefs characteristic of urban populations particularly useful (proposition 4). Chapter 8 traces the impact of the kind of institutionalization that accompanies a particular social change, the process of urbanization, on systems of belief.

The goal of this level of theorizing is to generate empirically relevant theoretical propositions that have application in diverse social settings. Although some of our statements may be worded so as to imply conviction, this does not mean they are all based on a well-established body of empirical evidence. Such evidence is hard to come by in cultural sociology, basically for the reason that clear expectations for results tend to evaporate in mists of vagueness and obscurity. Thus our apparent conviction is not certainty at all, but rather the by-product of our attempt to avoid vagueness.

Our bald propositions that appear as statements of fact should, therefore, be taken as hypothetical generalizations worthy of empirical investigation by virtue of their relevance to major problems in sociology and their logical connections with other propositions. Our references to the empirical literature on belief should not be taken as documentation but as illustration and explanation. During the inductive stage of inquiry, after all, findings are more useful as theoretical suggestions than as evidence.

The literature on belief and related topics is extensive. A total enumeration of specific empirical works is probably not possible, even if restricted to this century; the volume is simply too great. The number of more general analytical works is smaller and more manageable, however, and among these there is still smaller corpus of work in which belief is abstracted from its particular substantive manifestations. A highly abbreviated bibliography of contemporary works by social scientists which fall in this latter category would have to include at least the following: Berger and Luckmann (1966), Converse (1964), Douglas (1966, 1970), Geertz (1964), Harris (1968), Mannheim (1936), Nettler (1970), Rokeach (1960, 1968), and Scheibe (1970). This arbitrary selection certainly ignores many important works. Our Bibliography cites additional sources, but it is not meant to be exhaustive of the field or even of the ultimate source of the ideas which appear in this book; it is a list of specific references which the reader may find useful.

To forestall inappropriate expectations, let us comment on what *A Sociology of Belief* is *not.* It is not a survey of past work on the topic of belief and society; such histories are readily available elsewhere. It is not a discussion of the work of the "heroes"; these are also plentiful and easily found—moreover it becomes increasingly difficult to warm one's hands over Weber's bones. It is not a methodological guide to either empirical research or to theory construction; formalization is most appropriate in the later phases of scientific work. And it is not in the *engagé*, humanist, or unctuous traditions that seem to have dominated the sociology of knowledge and the sociology of religion for the last few years. It *is* an attempt to build substantive middle-range theory in the area we call the sociology of belief—substantive theory that will have utility in empirical research.

We also hope that this book will have utility as a primary or supplementary text in courses in social psychology, sociology, and political science which touch its subject matter.

All statements made by social scientists about the social bases of behavior apply to the behavior of the social scientists making the statements. By the same token all statements about the social bases of *knowledge* apply to the statements about *knowledge* and the social scientists making them. That is, all our work is self-referential and no matter how much more complex it makes things, self-reference cannot be escaped.[3] Thus, this is a book of beliefs about beliefs and constitutes an attempt by professionals to systematize and extend the territory of a given belief system, namely the classic tradition in sociology.

We thank the following publications and publishers for permission to quote from copyrighted material: *The American Sociological Review, Diogenes,* Doubleday and Company, Jossey-Bass and Company, and Oxford University Press.

We also thank Denise Thornton, Dorothy Weise, and Barbara Bible for typing various drafts of the manuscript.

The authors are equally responsible for the contents of this book and share either praise or blame equally.

James T. Borhek
Richard F. Curtis

University of Arizona
Tuscon, Arizona
August 1974

[3] To describe the social basis of an idea is not to impugn the possible truth of that idea. Therefore, when we make socially "determined" assertions about the social "determination" of ideas, we are not subject to the paradox contained in the statement "Everything I say is a lie."

The "social determination of ideas" is not the rigid dogma implied by the language and used as a straw man by amateur sociologists. It does not imply, for example, that there is a one-to-one correspondence between a group's average income and each member's belief concerning the form of life after death. We are concerned with a kind of relation which might better be called "resonance" than "determination." Beliefs concerning the virtue of self-denial resonate better with poverty than with wealth, but are not simply *caused* by poverty. This will be discussed in greater detail later. To say that ideas are "socially determined" is to say that the way in which ideas respond to events varies with the social organization of the group which carries the ideas. Thus the different ways in which a scientific discipline, a religious sect, and a political party respond to relevant events is not only the object of our inquiry but, because of the self-referential character of social science, a condition of it (see Gouldner, 1970:Part I).

Contents

A Sociology of Belief

Belief Systems In Human Society

One of the universal characteristics of culture is that a number of people share sets of linked ideas which persist over some period of time and to which people are committed. These *systems of belief* are neither fleeting perceptions, nor are they private fantasies. In very simple societies there may be only a few, but usually there are many; in urban societies the variety can be bewildering.

The characteristics of belief systems, which are discussed in Chapter 2, vary. They include the type and amount of linkage between the individual beliefs that form the system, the amount of commitment they ask for and are accorded, the degree to which the beliefs confront empirical reality, the degree to which the belief system is receptive to innovation, the degree to which the belief system is tolerant or antagonistic to its real or potential competitors, and the style of organization of the belief system.

Beliefs all exist in a social environment and are carried by some kind of social organization. Beliefs may be about almost anything: politics, art, religion, etiquette, martial arts, the nature of the world, procedures for finding out about the nature of the world, what is worthwhile or not, dirty or clean, godly or ungodly—anything. However different belief systems may appear, they are *all* shared, persistent, internally linked, and the recipients of commitment, and this is what makes them similar enough to study as a distinct type of behavior. Thus we are not talking about *either* religious or secular belief systems but about *both* as a general category of social phenomena.

Sociology is the study of society, not of politics, art, religion, and so forth. Students of religion have long recognized the importance of social conditions in affecting religious thought. The sociological problem is to explore the place of belief in the very nature of social life itself.

This chapter begins to attack the problem by defining belief systems, and by discussing the various parts or elements that go together to make them up. The next chapter classifies belief systems in terms of their most salient variable characteristics

DEFINING PROPERTIES OF BELIEF SYSTEMS. Before listing the properties that define belief systems in human society, let us emphasize a point to which we return in detail in Chapter 3. The referent of our term *belief system* is a set of linked ideas. It is *not* the particular set of beliefs held by any given person. We are talking about a supraindividual phenomenon—culture—not its manifestation in the beliefs, attitudes, or personal realities of the individual members of society.[1]

[1]Though much ink has been spilled on the metaphysics of individual versus group, the present issue is no more obscure than this: "Is that which two people agree about the same or different from what each thinks privately?"

A belief system is a set of related ideas (learned and shared), which has some permanence, and to which individuals and/or groups exhibit some commitment.[2] The conditions of permanence, commitment, and connectedness are *variable* characteristics through which we expect belief systems to be related to social organization. This definition excludes fleeting perceptions (or even shared experiences) that do not call forth personal attachments and that may be unrelated to other aspects of group life. Consider a man on a subway who perceives that his seat-mate's girdle is pinching her at the same moment he interprets the sway of the car to mean that the Colosseum stop, where he thinks folk singers might board the train, is coming up soon. This is culturally conditioned behavior, but we should not expect it to be governed by the kinds of laws we hope to investigate for three reasons: (1) the girdle-pinch image is symbolically unrelated to the anticipated music, (2) the experiences should not be expected to have important consequences on regular social behaviors because they will be over in a few moments, and (3) the man has no personal or emotional stake in the content of these observations or even in their accuracy, so the relevance for his personal or social life is minute.

A belief that *has* the appropriate properties, and through them social significance, is seen in the archetypical transvaluational statement: "The last shall be first." This statement has been remarkably permanent in human history, is always found in conjunction with other beliefs critical of the existing social order, and has occasionally become an important prop in the world view of large social groups.[3] Since people have allowed themselves to be martyred in the name of this principle, its connection to social organization is significant in ways the previous example was not.

[2]The term *ideology* appears infrequently in this book. As Geertz (1964) and others have pointed out, whatever meaning the term once had has been badly muddied. The word *ideology* has acquired pejorative overtones that are alien to our use of the term *belief.* Our usage of belief accords quite closely with that of Converse (1964).

[3]Mannheim (1936) wove his argument around the epistemological problems raised by transvaluational statements. Transvaluation is the process in which a belief system exactly inverts the current stratification system. "It is easier for a camel to pass through the eye of the needle than for a rich man to enter the kingdom of heaven."

Some form of this belief has appeared in a remarkable number of cultures over a long period of history and, to the best of our knowledge, it always appears in comparable places in the social organizations associated with these cultures. Transvaluations are understandably characteristic of groups that consider themselves oppressed. Although usually a lower-class or lower-caste belief, it is by no means always so. McCarthyism of the 1950s, Wallaceism of the 1960s, and Agnewism of 1968-1972, though not expressions of the dispossessed, nevertheless express the same resentment of established groups that is found in the Gospel according to St. John, evangelistic Protestantism of all eras, and the Shimbara revolution in Japan.

Personal commitment is one of the most observable and interesting features of a system of belief. The beginning student of human behavior is struck first by the strangeness of other people's ideas, and next by their persistence. As if recapitulating the history of social science, one is apt to begin by asking in wonder, "How can they believe a thing like that so *strongly?*" and later ask. "Do *I* have beliefs that are so fundamental I don't even recognize their existence?" If it were not for the fact of personal commitment, of course, belief systems could not have strong social consequences, and the sociology of belief would be an intellectual dead end.

Yet, *belief systems have an existence that is independent of the individual who experiences the commitment.* As noted above, the believer does not contain the belief system; in fact, he is unlikely to be aware of more than a small part of it and, knowingly or unknowingly, he must take the rest of the system *on faith.*[4] The sociologist of belief must step away from that part of the theory dealing with psychological mechanisms and examine the social significance of the connectedness of the belief system qua system. *Psychological mechanisms such as cognitive congruency may help*

[4]Converse (1964) has convincingly demonstrated that the individual believer is unlikely to be aware of more than a small part of the belief system, and often mistakenly at that. We show later that men often justify single beliefs or actions by reference to a larger system, which, if they only knew it, does not even exist. This situation is posed as a common condition of modern consciousness by Berger, Berger, and Kellner (1973).

explain individual commitment, but they do not necessarily explain the connectedness of a belief system in human society.

The life span of belief systems is also potentially longer than the life span of individual humans. The factors that determine which items of belief will be retained and which will disappear, what the logic connecting the different beliefs will be, and how what remains of the system will recombine with parts of other systems in a new synthesis, are not the same as the factors that determine the preferences of an individual. In short, individual psychology provides the elementary mechanisms through which belief is related to social organization, but there is far more to the story than a list of its mechanisms. It is the purpose of this book to detail this story.

Belief systems vary almost infinitely in substantive content. We are referring to a general type of social phenomena, not specifically to religious belief. We want to emphasize that belief may be viewed as a social process, and belief systems as phenomena that can have almost infinite variation in their actual content. Science, flying saucer cults, and "The Movement" all meet our definition. Individual perceptions, idiosyncratic variations on standard beliefs, "authored" sets of beliefs which have never gained a following, and "dead" beliefs about which nothing can be reconstructed except the words, do not.

The boundaries of belief systems are generally, although not always, undefined. Social boundaries, unlike physical boundaries, are not the natural edges of things. They are decision rules constructed for some social purpose. For instance, decisions as to who must pay city taxes and whose children must attend what school create social boundaries. Collections of beliefs do not generally have neat boundaries unless boundaries are constructed with some social purpose in mind, for instance, determining who is "in" and who is "out." For the most part, the existence of a clear boundary is a clue that social purpose is being served.

A common human practice, however, is to attribute clear and genuinely social boundaries to the power of differences in belief. Belief systems often *appear* to have clear boundaries when the separation is really between this group and that, and it is pretended that the common bond of group membership is the belief. Because the distinction is so hard to make in practice despite the fact that it is theoretically clear, we are not going to emphasize the distinction between boundaries of belief systems (based on their internal logic) and boundaries of social systems (based on group membership).

There is one type of belief system in which the boundaries are quite clear and to which what we have said above does not apply. These are belief systems in which the individual beliefs are tied together by a powerful logic. These will be discussed in greater detail in Chapter 2 under the heading "System."

ELEMENTS OF BELIEF SYSTEMS. The elements of belief systems presented below are a list of the types of statements which *could* comprise a belief system. Many of these elements are implicit understandings within most belief systems. Indeed, many belief systems are formally incomplete in that no real stance is taken, implicitly or explicitly, on some issues. We shall see later that the extent to which attention has been given to such matters—even the extent to which the collection of beliefs *is* systematic—is a *variable* characteristic of belief systems. The need for explication of the elements depends on the use to which the belief system is actually put.

Our emphasis on *systems* of belief is not meant to represent an analytic framework imposed by the investigator, but rather to represent an important characteristic of the way people use beliefs. The necessity for considering system is clear from the fact that out-of-context beliefs are meaningless. More importantly, when people use one or more beliefs, they adduce the system (whether it exists or not) to a variable degree.

If all the statements contained in a given belief system were spelled out in black and white they might include, at a maximum, the following seven elements. In any specific case, one or more elements may be missing. The elements are listed in the order that would be logically required for the understanding of a belief system. This does not imply priority in value or in a causal or historical sense. In fact, our experience is that belief systems generally seem to evolve starting with the last-named elements and working back toward the beginning of the list.

1. *Values.* Implicitly or explicitly, belief systems define what is good or valuable. We refer to "ultimate" values or goals here in the sense that they are the values in terms of which proximate goals are justified. Although we shall speak of goals and values as guiding behavior, "justifying" or "legitimizing" would usually be more appropriate. Values tend to be abstract summaries of the behavioral attributes which society rewards, formulated after the fact. Groups think of themselves, however, as setting out to do various things *in order* to implement their values. That is, values are *perceived* as a priori, when they are in fact a posteriori to action. This may be confusing to the observer, but this sequence of thinking facilitates social order. A course of action may be declared socially legitimate if it can be shown to "derive" from a collective value. In short, individual behavior that must take account of the interest of other actors is organized under a principle on which all the actors more or less agree. Consensus on commitment to such a principle allows almost automatic concerted collective action.

Having abstracted a value from social experience, a group may then reverse the process by literally deriving a new course of action from the principle. Thus the seeds of social change may be contained in a traditional belief system. At the collective level, this is analogous to the capacity for abstract thought in individuals and allows great flexibility in adapting to events.

Concrete belief systems often substitute observable social events for the unmeasurable abstract values to give the values immediate social utility. "The outward sign of an inward grace," for example, is an idea that facilitates social evaluation without compromising the theoretic nature of the idea of grace. In doctrinal Calvinism, salvation is predetermined by and known only to God, but actual churches can organize themselves according to a kind of theological operationalism: "by their fruits ye shall know them." In *The Protestant Ethic and the Spirit of Capitalism,* Weber noted for the Calvinists about whom he wrote that although the nature of the individual's predetermination was theoretically unknowable, success in one's calling came to be understood as a sign of election.

The substitution of concrete and observable social behavior for abstract and unmeasurable values frequently results in these values acquiring implications they did not initially have. For example, science may be taken as valuing expanded understanding; at the abstract level this may not imply the value of greater government expenditures on the space program, but at the concrete level it might entail exactly that derived value. In the case of *The Protestant Ethic,* cited above, Weber shows that a derived implication of the idea of "the outward sign of an inward grace" was that poverty is a sign of evil or damnation (failure at one's calling) and therefore no responsibility of the wealthy (those successful at their callings).

2. *Criteria of Validity.* According to what criteria is the determination of the validity of a statement to be made? At the abstract level, the institution of science uses logic and empirical truth with the implicit assumption that they ought to be compatible in the long run. Concretely, adjustments between the logic we understand and the events we can observe have to be made. A rigid, perfectionist insistence that all our methods be perfect before we speak would lead to silence and the death of science. In practice we allow a little of what pool players call "slop." Moreover, there are other criteria in actual scientific thought such as parsimony, elegance, and practicality.

In many belief systems, abstract criteria for validation of a statement have not been systematically explored, are totally implicit, or are subject to unannounced change. Mathematics is the most explicitly developed body of thought available to us, largely because the nature of invalidity—inconsistency—has been defined so clearly. Outside of mathematics one must often rely on concrete-level criteria (which usually come down to a matter of consensus within some authoritative group) or simply keep an open mind concerning the validity of a cultural product. The large number of procedures by which beliefs are validated are discussed in some detail in Chapter 6.

3. *Logic.* The logic (or, in a sense, *language*) of a belief system

consists of the rules which relate one substantive belief to another within the belief system. For example, $A = B + C$ and $D = E/F$ are unrelated algebraic assertions, but the rules of algebra clearly specify what is necessary to relate them. The logic of algebra is highly worked out and available to anyone with the basic skills necessary to make use of it.

Obviously it would be inappropriate to apply the logic of algebra to limericks, or the classical rules of harmony to ethics. The set of rules for relating the lines of limericks to each other differs from the rules for solving equations. In some fields such as science, the arts, ethics, and law, these rules may be worked out and very explicit. You can look them up in a book. More often than not, however, the logic must be inferred from regularities in the way a set of beliefs is used. The logic will be implicit, and it may not be consistently applied. The believers themselves may be ready to vociferously deny the statement that they are operating according to such and such a set of rules. An example of research in which the stated goal was constructing the logic for the use of a belief system can be found in Castaneda's *The Teachings of Don Juan: A Yaqui Way of Knowledge*, a work far too complex to abstract here.[5]

4. *Perspective.* The perspective, or cognitive map, may consist of nothing more than a classification or set of conceptual tools. Often it forms thought by calling attention to aspects of the environment through the classification itself. One group may classify the newcomer according to his cephalic and nasal indices, while another may inquire into his state of grace. A third may look up his batting average.

Central in most perspectives is some statement of where the belief system and/or the group that carries it stands in relation to other things, especially in relation to other groups and world views. Are we equals? Enemies? Brothers? Rulers? Along with this description of the external social environment is a description of the group itself, and the place of each individual in it. Are we the children of a demanding parent? Prophets in our own right? Usually this includes

[5]See Castaneda (1971; especially 199ff.) and Willer (1971:17-38) for one way of classifying logics, and Moore (1957).

a special status order, which may be totally unrelated to social rank in the larger society. One of the recent Grand Dragons of the Ku Klux Klan was a tire changer in a tire sales store. Such disparity of status is especially common in secret societies.

The perspective may be stated as a mythology. It explains not only *who* we are and *how* we came to be in cognitive terms, but also *why* we exist in terms of the values. Meaning and identification are provided along with cognitive orientation.

5. *Substantive beliefs.* Statements such as $V = GT^2$, My Redeemer Cometh, Black is Beautiful, and so on, comprise the actual content of the belief system and may take almost any form. They can be understood only in terms of the previous four elements: values, criteria of validity,language, and perspective.

Historically, of course, the previous four elements may have been built up around a substantive belief to give it meaning and justification. The individual believer is usually better able to verbalize substantive beliefs than he is values, criteria, logical principles, or orientation, which are apt to be the unquestioned bases from which he proceeds. A famous jazz musician, for example, was able to answer thousands of technical and substantive questions about his work, but when asked "What is jazz?" could produce only the classic answer for this type of question: "If you have to ask, you'll never know."

Investigation of the bases of thought usually occurs only among philosophers or other full-time specialists, or in response to a specific communicative difficulty stemming from unclear assumptions. But for the believer, substantive beliefs are the focus of interest. Only an academic could be concerned about a category of thought before he had an idea to put in it. Although the believer may assume the existence of a framework of assumptions around his thought, it may not actually exist. That is, the orientation he shares with other believers may be illusory. As long as the community of believers is able to behave socially, they may act as if there were such an orientation, even though it has yet to be developed. For example, consider almost any religious system. It seems clear that such systems evolve highly detailed and highly systematic theologies long after they come into existence and that they came into existence as a bundle of rather specific substantive beliefs. The believers interact, share specific consensuses, and give themselves a name. Then professionals work out an orientation, logic, sets of criteria of validity, and so forth. One thinks of Marx's famous remark, "Je ne suis pas un marxiste."

6. *Prescriptions and Proscriptions.* This includes action alternatives or policy recommendations as exemplified by Lenin's "What Is To Be Done?" (1937) as well as norms for behavior. A familiar example of this element of belief systems is the "statement-of-what-is-wrong" that appears in the literature of every social movement. Being closer than substantive beliefs to actual behavior, this category of belief is more subject to the buffets of reality than are the preceding and is often the part of the belief system which arises first or is the source of change in an existing belief system.[6] Marx wrote the *Communist Manifesto* first, for example, explaining and justifying it later in *Capital.*

Norms represent the clearest connection between the abstract idea and the concrete belief because they refer to behavior that is observable. They are most responsive to social conditions in being directly carried by the group through the mechanisms of social reward and punishment.

7. *Technology.* Every belief system contains associated beliefs concerning means to attain valued goals. Some such beliefs concern the legitimacy or appropriateness of means, while others concern only the effectiveness of various means. Technological beliefs are not used to justify or validate other elements of a belief system, although the existence of technologies may limit alternatives among substantive beliefs.

In belief systems that do not pertain to physical activities, the term *technology* takes on a somewhat novel meaning. In religion, for example, prayer and sacrament are means of attaining the goals

[6]We would argue that one of the primary sources of change in religious belief systems is the need to match official belief to the actual behavior of the members.

defined by the belief system, as are organizational strategy and tactics in political movements, and are therefore properly called part of the technology.

Because it concerns *doing,* technology is often the meeting ground for fundamentally different belief systems, often to the dismay of purists. There is a kind of pragmatic marketplace of beliefs, with the remarkable feature that specialists tend to be excluded by their expertise and the purity of their thought. Large religious revivals are perfect examples of this, as are large-scale social protest activities such as the antiwar moratoriums of 1969 and 1970. Compromise, agreement, and amalgamation follow, and syncretism is the order of the day. The popular evangelists, sacred or secular, have never been theoreticians or theologians and have always been eclectics. But when theologians debate, the outcome can be holy wars.

Technology commands less commitment from members than do the other elements; among members, technicians tend to be the least fanatic. In part, this follows from the definition of technology as providing means for the goals of a belief system. When means are elevated to ends, as often happens, "technicians" can become remarkably fanatic. But this is because they are no longer technicians.

Technology is also the least basic element in the logical sense. Causally, a change in technology may be responsible for changes in the logically prior elements of a belief system, as detailed in the familiar sociological theory of culture lag. But this occurs because technology can influence the life conditions of believers, thus forcing an adaptation in the belief system itself.

Adherents of different systems may therefore socially conflict at the level of technology with minimum threat to the belief systems concerned. Since performance criteria are maximally congruent in technology, the likelihood that some resolution other than violence may be possible is maximized. This is not to say that agreement is likely in an absolute sense. Think of a conversation among a hydrologist, a farmer, a water witch, and a believer in the effect of prayer on plant growth; harmony would be unlikely at best. Yet, their chances of agreement would be greater in a plant-growing contest than in a debate over basic philosophy.

We should point out here, however, that because it is public and visible, technology *may* become symbolic of more fundamental differences between belief systems and, therefore, a source of conflict. Thus, much blood has been shed between Muslims and Hindus over the fact that their religions have different and conflicting dietary restrictions. The conflicts are not over technology but over what technological difference symbolizes.

APPLYING THE DEFINITIONS TO CONCRETE BELIEFS. Identifying the elements of a belief system empirically is no easy matter, but we contend that this distressing fact is not to be taken as merely the fruits of bad theory. Sometimes the reason human behavior is hard to observe is that it has been deliberately concealed by those in question. As we indicate in the next chapter, this is often the case in the study of belief systems.

The true criteria of validity, for example, are often concealed from outsiders to legitimize various practices, or in order that the faithful may not be misled by their own belief system. The literacy tests for voter registration in Southern states were supposed to separate citizens competent to follow the affairs of state from those with inadequate access to information, but in fact they separated blacks from whites. In truth the relevant values were about race, not citizen awareness. Outsiders using the wrong criteria of validity cannot make convincing arguments to believers. A Ford salesman will never be convinced of the truth of Chevrolet's advertising claims by mere laboratory tests. *His* criterion is whether a car is a Ford or not.

Therefore the empirical study of belief systems has had to proceed with initially modest goals. Describing a belief system and identifying its elements is hard enough, and statements of the relationships among the elements (or of covariation between characteristics mentioned in the next chapter) is still more difficult. In any case, the bulk of empirical research on belief systems is still largely descriptive, perhaps for good reason.

The most promising area for even descriptive research, we think, is one that has received relatively little attention, namely the logic of belief systems.[7] Although we have cited only a few of the actual studies of this element, the field is not crowded and has great potential importance for other research. Certainly it is difficult to study the social dynamics of a belief system without understanding its inner logic, and this is the situation of most investigators.

SUMMARY. Belief systems are sets of related ideas which are learned, shared, more or less permanent, and the recipients of commitment by individuals and/or groups. They are aggregate phenomena and thus not reducible to the beliefs of any given individual, although their existence depends upon the maintenance of individual commitment. Our use of the term *belief* does not imply any specific type of substantive content—anything that meets the above definition will be called belief.

Belief systems are composed of types of statements, and although some may be implicit and some may be absent, a full list of the types of these statements would include: values, criteria of validity, logic (or language), perspective, substantive beliefs, prescriptions and proscriptions, and technology. As we observe in Chapter 6, validation in part depends on making a convincing show that the lower levels of these elements derive from the higher ones (substantive beliefs from values, for instance), whereas more often than not belief systems appear to evolve beginning with the lower level elements (technology, for instance) and working back up to the higher levels.

[7]In addition to footnote 6 above, see Mills (1940).

2.

To allow abstract generalization without imposing an artificial order on nature, we posit a relatively small number of variable abstract characteristics of belief systems which are of critical importance for the belief systems themselves and are logically independent of one another. A "type" is simply a description of the place a belief system occupies in the space defined by a number of continua. To the extent the characteristics are chosen properly they may be causally related, though the answer to this question is based on empirical research beyond the scope of this book. The problem of typology itself is discussed first in this chapter, after which we take up the variable characteristics of belief.

THE PROBLEM OF TYPOLOGY. Typologies bear close watching because they have important consequences for research. The descriptive language in terms of which a theory is stated and/or verified ought not to contain the conclusions of the theory. Basic assumptions and important relationships ought not to be hidden in the structure of a language itself. It is reasonably well agreed upon that whereas a language does not *determine* thought (non-Newtonian physics were discovered using Newtonian concepts, and so forth), it nevertheless may predispose thought in given directions by focusing attention. Therefore, typologies, which *are* descriptive languages, are important.

The polar typologies with which we are so familiar in sociology, such as gemeinschaft/gesellschaft, primary/secondary, and mechanical/organic, are a case in point. The folk-urban continuum, for example, does not actually *force* a student of the relationship between population size and occupational specialization to interpret a population increase as urbanization, but it certainly encourages the student to do so. That is, a *change* in population size tends to be interpreted as a *transition* from one polar type to the other, which could be factually false or true and still irrelevant. Similarly, an intermediate value tends to be seen as *between* the folk condition and the urban condition, which may be a useful observation in some contexts, but a misleading non sequitur in others. In this sense the traditional typologies tend to impose their own reality on nature, or at least to direct attention away from features of reality which may be important though missing from some particular theory—such as urbanization.

Consider Weber's typology involving inner worldly/other worldly asceticism/mysticism, for example. Its *general* utility is limited by the style of thought involved. Talcott Parsons, in his introduction to the 1963 translation of *The Sociology of Religion*, notes that such typological thought distracts attention both from intermediate values and from genetic properties. In addition, polar types focus attention on preconceived outcomes, both in suggesting answers to the questions "Where will it all end?" and "How did it begin?" which are distinctly not in evidence, and by implying the causal process according to which "It will get there," which is usually also not in evidence. And so if you apply Weber's typology to the religious movement on the corner, you may thereby understand what is making them other worldly and ascetic, but then you may be grossly misled, because your application is different from Weber's.

Parsons also suggests a step toward the proper utilization of Weber's typology—locating the variables that underlie it. Parsons interprets most of the book and its included typologies as an evolutionary theory of the rationalization of belief systems. This process consists in their symbolic development and systematization, the application of these more highly developed ideas to behavior in the form of "normative control," and the extension of commitment, in thought and action, to the ideas. The function of these variables, however, is still to inform the typology: to explain the meaning of "rationalization" in the transition from primitive animism to modern rational monotheism.

To locate a more generally useful system of classification, the relevant component variables must be abstracted from that particular sweep of history, or from that particular implied theory about the sweep of history, whichever the case may be. At a minimum, we must be able to think about combinations not available in the historical materials analyzed by Weber, including *un*systematic belief systems with little empirical relevance but great moral significance in urban societies. As Parsons points out, some such disentanglement of "independent variables" was one of Weber's unique goals. Abandonment of polar typologizing in favor of abstract description is a means to precisely that goal.

Far more than in the study of minerals, body types, personalities, or even social organizations, the necessary act of classification itself —when human beliefs are the object—seems to destroy the reality under investigation or to create a new, artificial order that does not exist in nature. It is a truism, of course, that any classification of data destroys something, even if only the rawness of the original data. The cost seems unduly high in the case of classifying beliefs. It is neither that belief systems are beyond analysis nor that existing analyses are incompetent, but simply that belief systems are substantively unique, and any useful typological effort ought to recognize this.

The paradox stems from the simultaneous dependence on, and independence from, the human organizational vehicle that carries belief. Belief systems, unlike rocks or animals, exist only through being carried by on-going groups of humans. While the groups' organizational problems affect the very meaning and significance of the beliefs, a system of belief has characteristics of its own which influence its operation and utility, independent of the group which carries it.[1] Thus, to abstract a belief system from its social context is to do violence to its meaning, but *not* to do so traps us into regarding all human situations as totally unique, denying their comparability and, as well, the possibility of generalizations concerning their abstract characteristics.

The solution to this apparent paradox lies in the manner in which the process of classification is understood. Butterflies may be classified by dividing the potentially finite list of insects into categories on the basis of similarity such that the members of any given category are so much alike that, in general, it is theoretically fruitful to state propositions that treat members of a category as if

[1]The genetic basis for classification in biology—categorizing units by their presumed familial relationships—tends to produce a useful structural basis for classification because inheritance is a central determinant of physical structure in animals.

they were identical. But the elusiveness of beliefs, based on their simultaneous existence *in* a social context and independence *from* it, prohibits the *general* utility of such categorization. The typological problem is more like that of trying to classify units of matter or energy: They have important abstract characteristics that may be related to one another, but to classify units of matter by similarity in size does not produce a typology in which members of the same class are especially similar in terms of color. *Beliefs, like units of mass or energy, should be thought of as things which have variable abstract characteristics, not as members of categories based on similarity.* By understanding the problem of typology as one of allowing statements of relationship among phenomena which vary along a finite number of dimensions but which are substantively unique, it is possible both to *describe* the vast variety of belief systems and to *generalize* about the relationships among characteristics of belief systems.

The apparent elusiveness of belief systems derives from four characteristics, all of which result from the fact that while beliefs are *used* by humans, they also have properties that are independent of their human use.

First, belief systems appear to their believers to have a stability, immutability, coherence, and independence from human agency that stems precisely from their use by human social organizations. To be of use for human purposes, that is, belief systems must be constructed to appear to group members as a suprasocial set of eternal verities, unchangeable through mere human action and agreed upon by all right-thinking people not because they (the verities) belong to a people but because they are TRUE.[2]

This stability makes belief systems appear far easier to classify into categories based on similarity than in fact they are. One is tempted to regard a belief system as being both as concrete and immutable as it pretends to be. In reality, beliefs are changeable. They respond to their embodiment and use by humans and they are generally not supported by complete consensus or even understanding.[3]

[2]See Schwartz (1970:6-7) and Durkheim (1965) for the classic statement.

[3]See Converse (1965:206-261) for some hard data on this point.

Second, genetic or familial similarities among beliefs are often interesting but they do not necessarily parallel structural similarities among belief systems.[4] Function (actual utility), however, is so loosely tied to the historical source of belief that historical (genetic) classifications tend to not provide useful classifications from the perspective of structure, use, or even current meaning. For example, the beliefs surrounding what we call "Japanese flower arrangement" and those involved in a mystical disengagement from contemporary sociopolitical institutions (selected and adapted borrowings from Zen) have the same historic roots but differ markedly in current meaning, function, implications, and significance. In fact, the former may represent a suburban mother's affluence, community status, and group affiliations, while the latter may represent her daughter's rebellion against them.

Third, the historic source of beliefs *may,* by virtue of their original use, endow them with features that remain through millenia of change and that particularly fit them to use in novel contexts. For example, Tibetan monks originally invented a system of self-defense (known to Americans as Ju Jitsu) to give unarmed pacifists the confidence to travel in small numbers through sparsely inhabited territory where armed bands of brigands might be encountered. The system was bound up in and (in some sense) logically derived from a philosophical and cultural system in which it was ethically important that the impetus of the attacker provided the means for his defeat.[5] In diffusion, the philosophical and cultural trappings as well as the function and social significance of the system of self-defense changed, while the logic of the system (its use of the attacker's own force to defeat him) remained relatively constant because of its utility. Japanese Samurai adopted and developed the system, thus allowing very small numbers of trained aristocrats to dominate masses of commoners by force of arms. During World

[4]We are referring here to an inner logic that may dictate to what problems the beliefs are germane, what procedures of validation are relevant, or what inferences must be drawn when believers are confronted with evidence from the outside world. On this point, see Moore, 1957; Schwartz, 1970: *in toto,* but especially p. 8; and Willer, 1971:17-18.

[5]*Encyclopedia Brittanica,* 1957, Volume 13:177, 179.

War II, the principles were incorporated into the training of mass armies and applied in the context of organized warfare. Today, television teaches Americans the same principles to give them the confidence to walk city streets.

Fourth, a classification of beliefs must abstract belief from the type of social structure which carries it, but the most important commonality among a set of beliefs is *precisely* the social structure. For example, the church-sect continuum or typology is a classification of social structures, but in its theoretic use it slides very quickly into a typology of belief systems and even into a typology of individual attitudes or orientations toward religion.[6] The ability to speak of "the type of belief system ordinarily carried by a sect" because such belief systems have important properties in common is highly useful, but (a) such a usage types social structures, not belief, and (b) such a belief system *may* be carried by a different structure, and a sect *may* carry a different type of belief system. Basically, the problem is that social organization and belief, the very objects between which it is important to state the relationship precisely, become entangled in the language (classification) used to refer to them.

Finally, there is enormous variety in belief and if the range of types is not infinite, it is certainly very large. In part, such variety results from an endless history of schism and syncretism as groups endeavor to distinguish themselves from, or identify themselves with, one another. Hence, a substantive typology of beliefs could be as long as history.

THE VARIABLE CHARACTERISTICS OF BELIEF SYSTEMS. The following discussion certainly does not exhaust the possible variable characteristics of belief but is intended to set a framework that can guide and be elaborated in empirical study. The choice of variables here is, to a considerable degree, arbitrary. We do not list the characteristics most often mentioned in earlier classifications

[6]In the sequence cited, Troeltsch (1931), Niebuhr (1957), Pope (1942), and Dynes (1955).

because, with the exception of that of Johnson (1963), those given when classifying on the basis of *similarity* are not relevant when classifying by abstract variables. We choose a given variable for the importance, in our evaluation, of its consequences for the belief system itself, and our evaluation was made on the basis of our experience with the empirical literature in this area.

System. Belief systems are not simply collections of norms which vary only in whether their substantive focus is religion, morals, politics, etiquette, appropriate research procedures, or love-magic. They are structures of norms which bear some relationship to each other and vary greatly in the degree to which they are *systematic.* What is systematic about belief systems is the interrelatedness of the various substantive beliefs. Some systems are more tightly interrelated than others.

At one end of the continuum are belief systems that consist of a few tightly linked general statements from which a fairly large number of specific propositions can be derived. Confronted by a new situation, the believer may refer to the general rule to determine the stance he should take. Science is an example of such a belief system. The principle of the experiment remains the same regardless of the differences in empirical problems to which it is applied.

At the other end of the continuum are belief systems that consist of sets of rather specific prescriptions and proscriptions between which there are only weak functional links, although they may be loosely based on one or more *assumptions.* Confronted by a new situation, the believer receives little guidance from the belief system because there are no general rules to apply, only specific behavioral laws that may not be relevant to the problem at hand. Such belief systems provide orientation only for specific situations. Religions that have evolved in agrarian settings are typically of this type, as are codes of etiquette. The prescriptions and proscriptions of belief systems with low system may be so concrete that they do not easily transfer to another cultural or subcultural setting. Of what utility is the peculiar American custom of switching the knife and fork from hand to hand in a Bedouin setting, where eating is done with the fingers of the right hand only and the left hand is ritually unclean? There is simply no level on which one is applicable to the other. By contrast, the rules of scientific method, being systematic, may be applied to all kinds of data without regard to their location. Thus, a high degree of system is in one sense an aid to diffusion of belief.

A high degree of system may, however, inhibit diffusion in another sense. It may make an otherwise useful trait inaccessible or too costly by virtue of the baggage that must accompany it. Zori (Japanese sandals) may diffuse without Japanese floors, but the convenience of subways entails an entire technology and a system of norms for its use.

System also has consequences for social control. To the degree that a system of beliefs is highly systematic, social control may be affected on the basis of informal sanctions and may be easily taught and learned. Belief systems with a relatively high degree of system seem to rely on rather general internalized standards to maintain social control—standards such as generalized codes of ethics (science) or guilt, which is associated with a whole category of behavior such as pleasure (Puritanism). To learn part is to learn all. Belief systems with relatively low system, such as agrarian religions or systems of etiquette, seem to depend on external sanctioning. The demand that believers refrain from eating meat on Friday, for instance, or that they identify their commitments through dress, mannerism, and ritual act, or that they leave the last bite of food on every plate are examples of such behaviors. This kind of behavior is, of course, demanded in some degree by all belief systems, and social control is always to a degree both internal and external. Relative weightings are different, however.

System is the most consequential of the abstract characteristics of belief because the greater the degree of system, the more relevant the other characteristics of a belief system are for one another. In a belief system such as a code of table etiquette or an agrarian religion that has a very low degree of system, a change in one characteristic has little relevance for a change in any of the others.

In any kind of belief system that has a high degree of system—a scientific theory, for instance—a change in one proposition requires adjustments in all others.

Functional analyses are based on the assumption that the parts of a system exist in a relationship of interdependence, a change in one part implying at least adjustments in the others. If what we have said above is true, then the assumptions of functional analysis are met only by belief systems that are highly systematic.

Empirical Relevance. By *empirical relevance* we mean simply the degree to which individual substantive beliefs confront the empirical world. The proposition that the number of times a cricket chirps per minute is a function of air temperature has high empirical relevance. It can be tested relatively easily. The proposition that whatever happens is all part of God's grand scheme of things cannot be tested in any human context and has low empirical relevance. Or, to take another example, how could an attitude of awe toward a sacred peak in a mountain range be proved or disproved by an event? Empirical relevance has consequences that have been noted by many politically interested commentators. To the degree that beliefs lack empirical relevance they shift attention away from problems in this world to problems in some other world, from political action in the here and now to some sort of ultimate triumph in the sweet by-and-by. When beliefs lacking empirical relevance arise in response to some pressing strain in the economic or political systems, collective action to solve economic or political problems becomes unlikely.

Belief systems lacking empirical relevance are sometimes called "escapist," but the choice of the word involves an oversimplification. Lack of empirical relevance probably stems in many cases not from escape but from an inability to see or handle complex problems that are nevertheless inescapable parts of reality. Cantril refers to "limited frames of reference" in this regard, meaning a set of conceptual tools inadequate (by virtue of lack of education, narrow cultural horizons, or anxiety) to handle the problem at hand.

Historically, it is probably safe to say that other worldliness has characterized belief systems that have arisen among powerless or uneducated groups in urban societies, or among preliterate peoples when faced by the uncontrollable and unpredictable forces of nature.[7]

Lack of empirical relevance also has another cause. Belief systems that are carried by a social vehicle that encompasses a heterogeneous population tend to become ritualized and to focus on relatively unempirical issues. In this case, lack of empirical relevance protects the belief system and its social vehicle from controversies arising between the highly differentiated population of believers. State religions—Roman Catholicism in Italy, or Lutheranism in Denmark—are perfect examples of such a social vehicle. However, note that when such belief systems are transplanted into *less* heterogeneous populations, they become *less* ritualized and unempirical, as did the Church of England, when it came to the relatively unurbanized and frontier United States and became the Protestant Episcopal Church.

There may be a substantial negative relationship between empirical relevance and system, our comments about scientific method notwithstanding. Highly formal theories in sociology have tended to lack empirical relevance, for example, while empirical research has generally not been guided by systematic formal theory (Gibbs, 1972).

Willingness to Take on Innovations. The degree to which belief systems accept or reject innovations varies widely. There may be an almost complete closure protected by elaborate bureaucratic safeguards, as in formal systems of law and in state religions, or an almost willy-nilly acceptance of novelties, which seems to characterize agrarian religious systems and which certainly characterizes the hip life-style.

The major consequence of variable degrees of the willingness to

[7]See Cantril (1941), Malinowski (1948), and Cohn (1961).

take on innovations is the ease with which belief systems adapt to changes in their social environment. Syncretistic belief systems adapt, by definition, through the process of cooptation or amalgamation with intruding belief systems, taking on characteristics of the intruder and fusing them with existing local beliefs. Beliefs that readily accept innovations of all degrees of system survive extreme changes in social environment—witness the history of Shinto in Japan and Ascetic Protestantism in the United States. Radically different in substance and system, both take on innovation with relative ease. On the other hand, Roman Catholicism has evolved a very closed belief system that requires elaborate bureaucratic procedures to institute change.

Tolerance. Belief systems vary in their tolerance of competing beliefs. Some accept all others as equally valid but simply different explanations of reality. Others reject all other systems as evil, and maintain a position such as the one found in revolutionary movements that maintain a person is "either part of the problem or part of the solution." "No salvation outside the church" is a good statement of the extreme position.

Tolerance seems to be independent of system and of the acceptance or rejection of innovation, although research may uncover a fairly strong relationship between rejection of innovation and intolerance. Syncretistic belief systems are generally tolerant. Agrarian religions do not, to the best of our knowledge, ever maintain that competing agrarian religions are wholly evil. The hip life-style of the 1960s, however, was both syncretistic and intolerant of its antitheses. It was and is defined, insofar as it can be given a concrete definition, by rejection of the "organization" life, suburbia, establishment politics, and "straightness." In this sense it accepts innovation, is unsystematic, and is intolerant.

Science accepts innovation, is systematic, and is intolerant. Much of the material scientists have produced for mass consumption consists of polemics against competing belief systems such as astrology, unidentified flying objects, folk medicine, and theological definitions of the nature of man and the creation of the world.[8] Much of the dispute *within* the sciences is between the proponents of one paradigm or another and has the flavor of disputes between religious systems (Kuhn, 1970). Although science takes on innovations as a matter of principle, it is not tolerant of its competitors. Within the fraternity we are not tolerant of our competitors, although we seek out innovations within our own speciality.

There would seem to be a fairly strong probability of a negative relationship between empirical relevance and tolerance, simply because the relevance of highly empirical beliefs to each other is so clear.

The relative degree of tolerance or intolerance has obvious consequences for the belief system. For one thing, it affects the ease with which the organizational vehicle may make alignments with other organizational vehicles, thus affecting both the power for which the organization may strive and the likelihood of the belief being compromised out of existence in the process of institutionalization. Second, it affects the social relationships of the believers—either cutting them off from nonbelievers or making it more likely that they will have contact with nonbelievers. The "peculiar people" belief, where seriously maintained, has had the effect of keeping some groups outside the mainstream for a considerable period of time.[9]

Degree of Commitment Demanded. Belief systems do not all demand the same degree of commitment from members, a characteristic that appears to be independent of system, empirical relevance, acceptance of innovation, and tolerance. It is not entirely independent of the type of social vehicle by which the belief system is carried, however, as we point out below in a discussion of the differences between elite and mass beliefs.

Commitment demanded can be quite different from commitment accorded. Commitment demanded varies from much to little.

[8]See Polanyi (1958:141, 168 and elsewhere).
[9]Schwartz (1970) has an extended discussion of such a case.

Revolutionary belief systems typically demand total commitment of the person to the system and typically institute procedures, such as "party" names, to both ensure and symbolize that commitment (Crossman, 1949). Withdrawing religious groups also typically demand total commitment; one cannot be a part-time Hutterite. Beliefs that are carried by organizational vehicles organized along military lines—what Selznick (1960) called organizational weapons—demand 24-hour a day commitment and reject or expel hesitant members. Reform movements, on the other hand, often encourage members to have very low commitment. They do not attempt to involve the entire life of the member, but are satisfied if they can significantly commit only his wallet. Some belief systems do not even provide an organizational vehicle to which the member at large could become committed if he so desired. An example is Moral Rearmament (Braden, 1949).

At the extreme low point in commitment demanded are the ethnic belief systems, which demand only self-identification as a member. Needless to say, in periods of ethnic persecution self-identification requires high commitment *on the part of the believer,* but this is a different issue.

The degree of commitment demanded has consequences for the persistence of the belief system. If a belief system demands total commitment and cannot motivate the persons to make this commitment, it is not likely to persist for very long. Intentional communities (utopias) have typically failed in large part for this reason. The "organizational weapon" cannot survive unless it can recruit and keep members who will accept the extreme demands the belief system makes.

The amount of commitment demanded also seems to be related to what happens when the beliefs are threatened with invalidation. Belief systems that demand low commitment fail or are invalidated slowly as beliefs drop from the believers' repertoire one by one or are relegated to some inactive status. Invalidation of the belief system demanding total commitment produces noisy apostates (Crossman, 1949). High commitment belief systems seem to become invalidated in a painful explosion for their members, and such beliefs are often replaced in the believer by an equally high commitment to a belief system opposing the original one.

Style of Organization of Beliefs.[10] Just as the internal parts of any social system are arranged according to some describable style, so are the internal parts of a belief system. The internal organization of a belief system is not entirely independent of the social vehicle which carries the beliefs, however. The two are inescapably linked, and some kinds of social vehicles absolutely demand that associated beliefs be organized according to a given style, as should become obvious below. The organization of the one is easily confused with the organization of the other, but it is the organization of *beliefs* that we are discussing here.

1. *The "Onion."* Some belief systems are organized as if in onionlike layers. Each layer, excepting sometimes the most superficial one, is systematic, intolerant, rejects innovation, and demands high commitment, but the layers may involve quite distinct substantive beliefs. The organizational weapon is a type case. The beliefs presented to outsiders may be substantively quite different from those held by low ranking insiders, which may in turn be substantively different from those held by members of the inner power-holding group (Selznick, 1960). The "layers" of belief parallel social cleavages in the organization that separate subgroups into varying degrees of power and commitment.

The least committed parts of such an organization are also those in which "outside" commitments must be reckoned with. Social mobility within the organization measures step-by-step rejection of "outside" values as well as heightened organizational commitment. This is the case with the Jehovah's Witnesses (Stroup, 1945; Cohn, 1955).

The onion form of organization is typically found in revolutionary groups within a hostile population, where it is to the advantage of the organizational vehicle to disguise its real purposes, where direct conversion of the population may be illegal, and where the

[10]The style of organization of beliefs is not a continuum; rather it is a set of commonly encountered empirical types. Our discussion is in some ways parallel to that of Rokeach (1968).

populace could be expected to respond with hostility to a direct statement of purpose.

The autobiographies of ex-Communist Party members in Crossman's book, *The God That Failed,* reveal this pattern. The Communist Party presented itself to the public at large as a friend of the worker, supporter of humanitarian causes, and the champion of oppressed minorities through the "Popular Front" of the middle 1930s. The members of local cells, whose stories form the book, believed not only in the expressed goals of the Party but in revolutionary overthrow of existing governments to achieve them, although they did not convey this part of their belief to the public at large. The invalidating experience that provoked defection from the Party was generated by the realization that the only inner circle belief was loyalty to the interests of the Soviet Union, and that the beliefs presented to them and to the public at large were simply tools in the struggle for power and did not involve even passing commitment to the stated goals of the "Popular Front."

2. *The Front.* The front is really the outer layer of the onion. Some belief systems are tools used to impress, delude, or attract a public by an organization whose real purposes are hidden and expressly kept from view. Two examples already given are the "Popular Front" and the evangelism of the Jehovah's Witnesses. Another example of the front—a most unfortunate one—is the typical introductory course in a university curriculum, which bears little or no similarity to what academicians really believe and the kinds of problems upon which they really work.

The organization of the front involves low demand for commitment and total subordination to inner levels of the organizational vehicle. Although the front is often thought of as a purely political animal, obvious examples can also be found among medical or pseudoscientific belief systems that are generated and supported by a hidden organization with the intent to play upon ignorance and defraud the public.

3. *The Stratified Belief System.* Probably the two most familiar styles of organization for belief systems are the stratified belief system and the folk belief system. In stratified beliefs, system, empirical relevance, acceptance of innovation, tolerance, and

commitment may vary but access to the belief system is a process in which the believer must pass through successive layers of belief. In Masonry, for instance, attainment of one layer is a prerequisite to attainment of the next, but the stratification seems to have as its purpose identification of social status. Rather than being the intellectually necessary prerequisites to the ones following, the layers are ritual barriers to attainment of the desired status. The same is probably true of all secret societies, and graduate students are fond of saying that it is true of Ph.D. programs. In science, mathematics, and logic, the layers are necessary prerequisites to further attainment, although it is not necessarily the case that in all such instances the layers are ordered in terms of complexity.

The distinction between an onion and a stratified belief system lies in the function the layers play for the total system. The social "problem" addressed in the onion is insider versus outsider; that addressed in a stratified belief system is rank within the organization. The outer layer of belief in an onion protects or provides a sort of belief buffer zone between wholly committed insiders and uncommitted outsiders. The top of a stratified belief system is more esoteric, more inclusive, more difficult, or "purer" than the bottom. In practice, the distinction between the two can be quite confusing because an organization carrying a stratified belief system may, in fact, use its lowest level of belief as a buffer to outsiders as if it were an onion. Frequently enough, high ranking academicians are less competent at teaching introductory courses than barely initiated graduate students. Indeed, the practice of staffing introductory sections with graduate assistants probably protects *both* the outsider and the high ranking insider.

4. *The Folk Belief System.* Folk beliefs involve low system, variable tolerance, and low demand for commitment. Empirical relevance may vary but it is, in our experience, usually high. They closely approach a random assortment of norms organized only on the basis of locality and tradition. There may be stratification of belief on the basis of age, sex, and social status, but access to such beliefs is a consequence of the believers' location and social status, whereas in a stratified belief system, social status is a function of the believers' attainment of one or another level or kind of belief.

5. *Elite and Mass Beliefs.* Many historically important belief systems are bifurcated into two related and parallel subsystems, one for the mass and another for the elite. The distinction between mass and elite beliefs is more complex and subtle than a distinction between "real" and "ideal." Weber, for instance, remarked on the difference between the Confucianism of the elite, which was ethical and this-worldly, and the Confucianism of the masses, which was magical and highly concerned with ancestor worship (Bendix, 1960: 134-151). "Maryolatry" or "Maryism" is a mass belief system within Roman Catholicism in which the Virgin Mary assumes an importance she does not have in official theology.

The two belief systems are parallel but slightly different. In the practice of democratic politics, the beliefs of the public seem at considerable difference from the beliefs of professional politicians. Elite and mass beliefs differ according to complexity, certainty, and response to failure. These can be seen as evidence of the pressure on a single belief system generated by contrasting social conditions.

Elite belief is conceptually more complex than mass belief. The number and subtlety of distinctions is greater, the time perspective is longer, and whatever system of categories classifies "ins" and "outs" is more complex. In mass belief, time perspective is typically a great deal shorter than in elite belief; that is, the outcome of the final struggle between the forces of light and the forces of darkness is made to seem immediate, whereas in elite belief it is generally deferred to some indefinite time in the far distant future. Stereotype in its crudest forms is a characteristic of mass belief. An elite is far more likely to stereotype an organization while bearing its actual members no ill will.[11]

The conceptual system of mass belief tends to phrase the unfamiliar in terms of the familiar. Scientology, for instance, is reputed to make use of an analogy between the human mind and a computer, using fashionable terms such as *program* and *clearing* to describe complex cognitive processes. Popular theology has always personalized deities. The idea of the Holy Trinity is a far cry in complexity from "There ain't no flies on Jesus."

The degree of unequivocality and certainty is higher in mass than

[11]See Lanternari (1963), Lipset (1960), and Cantril (1958).

in elite belief. Cohn (1955) points out that in the archetypical example of angry mass belief, the Proletarian Movement, the outcome of the conflict is a foregone conclusion, as is the sadistic punishment to which the loser will be subjected. Final victory will bring a state in which the winners will be relieved of problems of age, illness, and all the other human miseries as well as have the fruits of political victory.

Mass belief and elite belief seem to react differently to negative evidence. A threat to mass belief is likely to result in scapegoating and a search for a new, conceptually simple belief that will provide again the lost certainty (Parsons, 1954).

6. *Specialized Belief Systems.* Another type of organization for belief systems requires each believer to show detailed familiarity with only one or two segmented aspects of the entire, complex system of belief. Specialties are connected by their clear relationship to a single, general body of belief or knowledge. An ornithologist, for example, may be woefully ignorant of mammology, marine biology, or invertebrate paleontology, but the body of general theory and method in zoology makes them all accessible to him and also coordinates his work with that of scholars in those specialties.

Bureaucratic social organizations frequently carry belief systems of this nature, not only in cases of complex bodies of doctrine, as in Roman Catholicism, but also in cases of a complex division of labor dictated by an industrial process or of imperative social control, secrecy, or the coordination of persons who differ from one another in various ways. The "need to know" may be defined bureaucratically from above; for example, sophisticated weapons may be developed by teams composed of many technicians, only a few of whom know what the weapon is or what it is for. The "need to know" may, however, be imposed by the believer himself, in terms of what is directly relevant to his daily life, for example.

The discussion of the style of organization of belief systems points to a problem which has been researched relatively little. Several versions of a belief system, which may be quite different, may be attached to a social vehicle that carries beliefs. The "onion" and the "front" are extreme examples of this. The front is, of course, the result of rather conscious dissimulation and has been characteristic of a number of religious groups in hostile environments and of espionage agencies everywhere. Even within highly established organizations operating in a receptive environment, however, different versions of a belief system may exist, carried either by different status groups within an organization—scientists working in industrial concerns or intellectuals working in labor unions, for instance—or by differentially recruited persons, such as converts in an established religious denomination.[12]

THE USES OF BELIEF, INCLUDING THIS TYPOLOGY. The dimensions of belief suggested above, including system, empirical relevance, acceptance of innovation, tolerance, degree of commitment demanded, and style of organization (and others, perhaps) can be cross-classified to form a typology or classification. More properly, any belief system can be abstractly described in terms of these dimensions.

What good is such a device? It is hoped that this typology would serve to facilitate thought and empirical research on the relationship between social organization and systems of belief. We expect it to be a useful scheme for classification because it comes to terms with the paradox that renders belief systems elusive: Human organizations carry and embody systems of belief, thus giving them life and necessarily affecting their development, yet belief systems also contain an inner logic that has implications independent from the social vehicle, and that may even operate to alter the social vehicle itself.

This would follow from the general proposition that *belief systems are more or less useful for a given purpose, depending upon their characteristics qua belief systems.* We offer this proposition as a potentially useful hypothesis in the sociology of belief. Just as the physical characteristics of an end wrench make it particularly useful for some purposes (such as moving nuts of a given size) and incidentally useful for others (as a paperweight), beliefs may be turned to different purposes by design or coincidence.

[12]See Wilensky (1956), Kornhauser (1962), Gouldner (1960), and Borhek (1965).

One line of theory in the sociology of belief will doubtless be based on the social utility of belief systems, and will therefore require certain qualities of the typology presented here: (1) Types must not be defined by the uses to which they are put. (2) Widely disparate belief systems must be comparable without undue loss of substantive uniqueness. (3) The characteristics of belief systems must nonetheless be relevant to social use, and to human adaptation to humans as well as to external circumstance. (4) The current use of beliefs must be separable from their historic genesis. (5) It must be possible to abstract belief from the type of social vehicle which currently carries it.

A typology in terms of general abstract characteristics, such as this one, breaks down substantive distinctions, for example, religion, politics, and so forth, and makes possible comparisons between substantively different belief systems. Whether the present scheme adequately bears these qualities, or not, it will prove successful if it provokes someone else into presenting a conceptual scheme that will do the same thing more adequately.

SUMMARY. Classifying or typing beliefs seems both necessary and difficult. Many attempts have been made to create classificatory devices, but with few exceptions they have not been particularly successful. We regard the problem of typology as a problem in relating phenomena which vary along a finite number of dimensions, but which are substantively unique. A "type," then, is simply a description of the location of a given belief system on a number of critical dimensions on which all belief systems may be expected to vary. These dimensions include: system, empirical relevance, willingness to take on innovations, tolerance, degree of commitment demanded, and style of organization of beliefs. This typology differs from others in the general area of belief in that it is in terms of variable abstract characteristics rather than in terms of similarity. We suggest that typologizing beliefs in terms of variable abstract characteristics is necessary; otherwise one is typing social structure rather than belief.

Belief as Culture

The basic assumption for a sociology of belief is that belief is a cultural phenomenon. Much of the sociological perspective on knowledge can be summarized in this statement. This chapter provides an abbreviated outline of the implications which follow from the statement that belief systems are part of culture. First, however, a major alternative posture, namely that belief systems are shared aspects of individual mental states, is briefly described.

SOCIOLOGICAL AND SOCIAL PSYCHOLOGICAL MODELS OF BELIEF. There are many ways to skin any theoretical cat. Although academic theorists are prone to defend their own positions as if they were Revealed Truth challenged by the forces of Ultimate Darkness, the fact of the matter is that a number of quite different and quite adequate theoretical models of a given phenomenon may exist at once.[1] Each will have its own virtues and shortcomings and each will direct attention to different problems and different aspects of the thing being studied.

The theoretical position we defend is that belief systems are cultural in nature, implying that belief is an aggregate rather than an individual phenomenon and must be viewed as existing independent of any given believer. The relation between the individual and the belief is expressed most aptly by Mannheim:

> Strictly speaking it is incorrect to say that the single individual thinks. Rather it is more correct to insist that he participates in thinking further what other men have thought before him. He finds himself in an inherited situation with patterns of thought which are appropriate to this situation and attempts to elaborate further the inherited modes of response or to substitute others for them in order to deal more adequately with the new challenges which have arisen out of the shifts and changes in his situation. (1936:3)

Belief has an independent reality over and above any given believer or combination of believers. This is not to say that belief systems are independent of believers and exist in some sphere of "essences" or have life in the sense that an organism does. Without believers there exists no belief system; but the belief system itself is not coextensive with any given individual or set of individuals. Belief systems have potentially longer lives than individuals and are capable of such complexity that they would exceed the capacity of a given person to detail. Belief systems, like all culture, have the peculiar quality of being real and having consequences but having no specific location. For Durkheim, the social power of belief lay in

[1]See Kuhn (1970) for an analysis of the nonscientific character of scientific revolutions. "Objectivity" in science is often simply a matter of whose ox is being gored.

its *external* quality—it seemed to believers to transcend the groups that carried it.[2]

For us, then, belief is a social fact that in Durkheimian dogma requires explanation by other social facts—which is to say that we are not interested in the individual's motive to believe any more than Durkheim was interested in the individual's motive to suicide. Everyone who commits suicide may be presumed to have some motive, though it may vary, but people in some categories (and in some particular social environments) are statistically much more likely to kill themselves than other people are. In the same sense, individual believers may be presumed to have some motive to believe, and yet major upheavals in belief have always been associated with major social upheavals: industrialization, economic disaster, military defeat, and so forth.

Our emphasis on the phenomenon of commitment does not imply that we are primarily concerned with what motivates individuals. Commitment is in some respects the central problem of a sociological analysis of belief. The fact that our theoretical model of belief is sociological means that we will focus on those aspects of social organization which maintain or create commitment—for example, limitation of alternatives, social isolation, and social insulation through strategies that dictate heavy involvement of the individual in group-centered activities. Our analysis of the process in which belief systems are validated or invalidated focuses on the supraindividual phenomena that create validation. These phenomena include the existence of certain kinds of strains in the social vehicle's environment, the belief system's ability to defend itself against disconfirming events, and the degree to which the belief system is affected in whole or only in part by a disconfirming event. A social psychological model of belief would treat these issues in a quite different manner, as we point out below.

The fact that belief systems are carried by social vehicles that are themselves embedded in a social environment raises a whole set of

[2]Durkheim (1965) is the classic source of this perspective. See Durkheim (1964:Chapter 2), Swanson (1966), and Mannheim (1936) for other classic statements of this same general position.

questions peculiar to sociology. What are the effects of organizational growth itself on belief systems? What are the mutual limitations of belief on organization and of organization on belief? And, of course, the familiar question about social movements: Why is it that success is always failure?

In sharp contrast to a sociological model of belief, psychological models begin with the individual. If they treat aggregate phenomena such as institutionalization at all they do so as if it were the sum of the behaviors of individuals. This is not to imply that they are incorrect, or that one cannot construct a social psychology concerned primarily with the specific mechanisms through which the individual and society influence one another. Rather, we want to emphasize that these types of theory attack different problems from the ones that engage our attention, even though many issues appear to be quite similar.

Rokeach, one of the major contributors to a social psychology of belief, defines a belief system as "having represented within it, in some organized psychological but not necessarily logical form, each and every one of a person's countless beliefs about physical and social reality" (1968:2). Included in the term *belief*, therefore, is something that has importance to and is held by particular individuals.

In an essay on the sociology of knowledge, written in what is generally called the phenomenological tradition, Berger and Luckmann define the "foundations of knowledge in everyday life" as "the objectivation of subjective processes (and meanings) by which the intersubjective commonsense world is constructed" (1968:2). In other words, people make their inner feelings become real for others by expressing them in such things as votes, statements, and edifices they build or tear down, which in turn form the basis of cooperative (or uncooperative) activity by humans, the result of which is "reality" (1968:45-118). Belief is one kind of reality although not all of it.

In this general framework, belief is to be studied in terms of the motivations, ideas, and attitudes of individuals and the way individuals put them into action. If belief has any reality over and above individuals it is treated as it *affects* individuals. Berger and Luckmann treat the maintenance of what we have called social facts as a problem in maintaining the commitment of the individual to an established reality, that is, they focus on mechanisms that convince persons.

The basic assumption of the reality construction school in sociology, that interacting humans affect the "realities" which in turn affect their interacting, is unobjectionable enough. We could scarcely agree more. This position offers two dangerous pitfalls to the unwary, however. The first is that it tempts one to fall into building Adam and Eve myths. Taking the word "construction" literally may lead to the building of pseudohistories of the type commonly encountered among preliterate peoples who "construct" a history involving mythological figures or animals that is plausible in the context of their culture and that "accounts for" how things are today. Such constructed histories may be plausible to the people who construct them but they are unempirical in the extreme. Berger and Luckmann (1968) are quite aware of this danger and yet still succumb to it. Much of their argument is about *A* and *B* or Crusoe and Friday or some other completely unempirical variation on the Adam and Eve theme.

The second danger in reality constructionism, and all of what is commonly called symbolic interactionism for that matter, is clearly portrayed in the familiar fairy tale, "The Emperor's New Clothes." There really are individuals in nature busy at the work of attempting to construct reality—usually to their own benefit—such as the fraudulent tailors of the fairy tale, and that "reality" has consequences: The emperor, his court and the townspeople were pleased with the new suit of clothes. But there is always a wise child or suspicious investigative reporter who will shatter the "reality" by observing that the emperor is nude. The moral of the story is not that guilt will out, in the end, but that there is another reality out there—partly constructed, in its own way, out of human interaction—against which the wares of Acme Reality Construction, Inc., may be compared.

Reality is not constructed, as Madison Avenue would have it; reality is encountered and then modified. Humans do, in fact, encounter each other in pairs or in groups in situations that require them to interact and to develop beliefs in the process. They do so, however, as socialized beings with language, including all its implicit values, logic, and prescriptions or proscriptions; in the context of the previous work of others; and constrained by endless social restrictions on alternative courses of action. The paucity of empirical examples drawn from real life in Berger and Luckmann (1968) follows quite possibly from the fact that none exist. "Constructed realities" are more apt to be found in television commercials than in real life. How many families achieve virtual satori because Mom has switched to a new margarine?

Theories of reality *modification* employ a more complicated model of causation, which presupposes a social reality that is not the same as the set of individually perceived personal realities. One of the best known such theories in the sociology of knowledge, for example, refers to the relation between ideas and their social uses as "elective affinities." It is presented most self-consciously in Stark's *The Sociology of Knowledge* (1958:256-263), though its best empirical presentation is in Weber's essay, "The Social Psychology of the World's Religions" (Gerth and Mills, 1958:267-301). Elective affinities is a model of the selection and adaptation of beliefs which states, essentially, that social groups "elect," from among available alternatives, beliefs for which they have an "affinity" on the basis of shared interests, conditions of getting a living, dominant life problems, and so on. They then modify these beliefs to suit *changes* in interests, conditions of getting a living, and dominant life problems.

The discussion of causation, by those who would explain social facts by social facts, is often unnecessarily mysterious. The model of causation we employ (discussed in greater detail in Chapter 5), is simply a loop in time. For example, a belief system is elected and modified for contemporary use by a group, which subsequently changes its organization because of the logic of the belief system, after which the reorganized group modifies the belief system to cope with some problems stemming from the new organization, and then the logic of the belief system leads the group to attack some new task, and so on. The fact that A affects B during one time period is not contradicted by the fact that B affects A during the next time period.

The fact that beliefs are not mechanically connected to organizations should call for no great mystery about the causal relations among ideas and groups. There are many possibilities, and none excludes the others. For example, people often use ideas as tools, so that the relation between an idea and a "function" need be no less causal, nor any more mysterious, than the relation between screwdrivers and changing tires. Groups respond to reinforcement schedules, so that if they receive rewards or escape punishments as an apparent consequence of holding a particular belief system, a collective learning model of causation would be quite appropriate without denying the fact that ideas are often used as tools. An evolutionary model would also be appropriate, if it could be shown that societies regularly died or disintegrated when they no longer perpetuated beliefs of a given sort.

The issue of commitment also arises in a social psychology of belief but is approached quite differently. In general, social psychologists have viewed individual commitment as stemming either from learning and reinforcements for what is learned, or from the fact that belief functions to maintain personality either by compensating for some feeling of inadequacy, by providing an object for dependence, or by producing order out of disorder.[3] Commitments are validated (or made legitimate) by mechanisms that make them subjectively meaningful to persons (Berger and Luckmann, 1968:85).

Social psychological frameworks also dictate some problems about which we would have nothing to say. Rokeach, for instance, invests a good deal of effort on the problem of the structure and change of individual belief systems (1968:21). This in turn dictates that he must concern himself with the problem of the relative importance of one belief or another to individuals, two issues of no importance in our framework.

In summary, the study of belief may be approached in a number of ways, each of which will dictate that one must be concerned with some things and may ignore others. Our examples were drawn from social psychology, but almost any other social science discipline would have served. This is not an eclectic compendium of facts

[3]See Allport (1954:271-272), Wallace (1966:13-39), and Fromm (1941).

about beliefs but an attempt to explore certain lines of theory. One of the most fruitful is simply the realization that the phenomenon commonly referred to as belief has the properties of Durkheim's "social facts."

CULTURE: THE SOCIOLOGICAL MODEL. Culture consists of learned (as opposed to innate) and shared (as opposed to truly idiosyncratic) ideas (as opposed to physical artifacts). At the outset, this definition may be taken to mean that the cultural sociologist excludes from the domain of things he will attempt to explain whatever is not shared by different people or whatever is shared only by virtue of biological or physical necessity. This definition of culture attributes the explanation for the *sharing* of certain beliefs to a certain kind of social process, the description of which is the regular business of general sociology. The process that accounts for the *acquisition* of culture by individuals is called *socialization* and consists of regular schedules of reinforcement.

At the simplest level, then, the assertion that beliefs are cultural rejects a whole range of possible alternate propositions. First, it rejects naive realism, the proposition that beliefs are more or less accurate photographs of reality and that what is problematic is their accuracy. One does *not* believe in the heliocentric orbit of the earth nor in the Immaculate Conception because they are intuitively obvious and derive without effort from a confrontation with the outside world. The explanation for the popularity of long hair is *not* its intrinsic beauty and the explanation for the near universality of the incest taboo is *not* its moral rightness, any more than the explanation for the popular awareness that $E = MC^2$ is its truth. Ideas may be good, true, or beautiful in some context of meaning but their goodness, truth, or beauty is not sufficient explanation for their existence, sharedness, or perpetuation through time. If this is still in question ask yourself, first, what the velocity of light is and, second, how you know that this is so.

More importantly, the assertion that beliefs are a part of culture brings all that sociologists have to say about the relation between social organization and culture to bear on beliefs. This makes possible the generation of a whole new series of propositions about the relation between belief and social organization, which in turn generates new series of propositions about social organization itself, as shown in the following example. In any social group there is a high probability of a negative relationship between role differentiation and consensus. That is, the more complex the group is, the less likely is consensus. If belief in an afterlife is part of a culture, then application of this generalization would lead us to expect that members of a given rural community should show more consensus about afterlife than members of a given urban community in the same society, although they might disagree, of course, with members of a different rural community. In addition to explaining the distribution of beliefs in a society, this application leads to a further generalization about social organization. Sanctions for a given behavior derived from a belief in an afterlife would produce greater uniformity with respect to that behavior in rural than in urban settings in the same society.

To go beyond what can be derived directly from the definition of culture requires some additional remarks. The rest of this chapter is devoted to describing the general theoretical orientation on which the sociology of belief is based.[4]

Culture is patterned. It consists of related, not discrete, elements which are organized according to some general pattern. To move a trait from one culture to another is usually to change its function and significance through "reinterpretation." This involves placing the trait within a novel context of meaning; thus, a piece of Persian armor has been transformed into the ubiquitous symbol of middle-class employment, the necktie. Likewise, to speak of *one* belief is to rob it of some of its meaning because it is a part of an entire cultural context. Humans, however, often communicate about beliefs as if they were separate particles and recognize the need for context only when communication fails. Politicians take great care never to

[4]Rather elaborate classifications of culture and orientation are available. See, for instance, Parsons and Shils (1951: Part 2) to whom our present orientation is heavily indebted. Our theoretical goal here is to simplify the orientation to the smallest number of terms required for analytic use later in this work. Obviously, it should be possible to add to our analysis by multiplying distinctions and building upon them in a substantive context.

announce an opinion without carefully describing its connection to traditional values.

The internal consistency of culture often escapes notice; it becomes apparent only when it is violated. One of the consequences of the organization life-style which attracted so much sociological attention during the 1950s was that it pointed out that large numbers of people were conducting their lives according to a set of norms wildly at variance with the dominant normative emphasis on work, economic and consumer individualism, and suspicion of hedonism.[5] In like manner, the hip life-style of the 1960s pointed up, through the response that it at first received, the remarkable intolerance of American culture to "other" life-styles.

Culture provides orientation. Culture is used by humans, individually and collectively, as the primary source of solutions to the problem of orientation. As we see later, culture may provide solutions to myriad substantive problems as well, but first and foremost it is the source of orientations according to which problems may be met with traditional and acceptable solutions. Whatever emergency you face, you will think about it in terms of time (conceived in years, days, minutes, and seconds), direction (north, south, east, and west), distance (miles, feet, inches), color (red, yellow, blue, and their combinations), and so on. Carriers of a contrasting culture might surmount the difficulty equally well but their orientations could be markedly different.

Hopi-speaking Americans, for instance, reputedly cannot cut time up into a series of instants because the machinery for this operation is lacking in their language. Polynesians do not cut the color spectrum up into the same pieces that Westerners do. It is traditional to assert that Orientals are more inclined to a passive and acceptant view of fate than Westerners; Max Weber traced out massive consequences of this difference in culture, as did Ruth Benedict.[6]

Culture provides quite different kinds of orientation to a social

[5]See Whyte (1957) or Riesman, et al. (1950). The most widely known discussion of the patterning of culture may be found in Benedict (1969).

[6]See Benedict (1969), Whorf (1956), and Bendix (1960:103-217, especially 151-157 and 213).

object all at once. The existence of one or more types of orientation is often so implicit that the people involved would not ordinarily recognize them without being prompted. Being academics, we found it natural to present examples mainly of cognitive orientations in the paragraph above. But, in addition to thinking, humans are regularly oriented in the business of feeling, evaluating, and doing (or being). These aspects or orientation to social objects are analytically separable, but one of the most interesting propositions in the sociology of belief is that social life tends to mix and confuse them; examples are organ preludes, starched collars, and a feeling of sanctity, or centers of learning, Saturday afternoon violence, and brass band music.

Culture changes in response to the pressure of events but only very slowly because it is to a degree systematic. That culture is systematic means that the goals, norms, values, and orientations it contains are linked and that a change in one has strong but subtle implications for change in others. Consider the peculiar resistance to the music of the twentieth century found in the Soviet Union—the cloud under which Shostakovich lived for a while and the anachronistic character of the work of Schedrin, not to mention the treatment accorded contemporary writers. Change is there but it is resisted because there is a perceived entanglement between aesthetic style and political loyalty.

As a set of solutions to substantive problems, culture is subject to immediate pressures for change. Besides providing in the first place the basic tools for any thought, feeling, judgment, or action, culture includes specific prescriptions and proscriptions, sets of rules on what to think, feel, and do. When these norms fail to solve practical problems, some alternative must be sought at once. Americans may, for example, adopt the metric system one of these decades because the English system is inconvenient, but the pace of this cultural change will not be said to have been headlong.

The theory that norms and values change less rapidly than technology is known as the theory of culture lag.[7] We should like to call it to attention here, emphasizing that systematic connections

[7]See Ogburn (1950).

between norms and values on one hand and technology on the other are a mechanism of the change. Commitment to norms and values is stronger than commitment to technology, in part because the technology is more closely geared to daily necessity. One of the commonplaces of courses in world population is that while it is easy to export technological knowledge that will result in a drop in the death rate it is extremely difficult to export knowledge that will help alleviate the population explosion that a drop in the death rate produces. In one case, only technology is involved; in the other case, basic social norms and beliefs are involved.

Cultures are differentiated into subcultures which are coextensive with networks of communication. That culture is coextensive with a network of communication follows from its definition. If societies consisted of homogeneous collections of persons, each communicating equally with all the rest, both culture and society would be undifferentiated unities. Since societies are differentiated, cultures are too, and along the same lines. The first job sociologists of knowledge set for themselves was to show that social cleavages (social class, ethnic group, region, occupational situs, age, and so on) are paralleled by cultural differences. Social movements, for example, arise along the lines of such cleavages and then fragment when their membership becomes sufficiently heterogeneous to include substantial representation in more than one major status or economic group. Causation can operate in both directions: an ideological schism often results in a break in the communication network which, in turn, allows the development of relatively distinctive subcultures. The history of Protestantism demonstrates this rather neatly.

Neither societies nor the cultures they carry are as simple as a set of discrete building blocks. Each member of a society participates in a somewhat different set of cultural "worlds," each consisting of shared meanings and extending as far as a system of communication can support it.[8] The cultural world of baseball is not coextensive with the male sex, the working class, or the 15 to 25 year age group, but involves a special terminology, shared status symbols,

[8]See Blumer (1962) and Manis and Meltzer (1972) for development of this point and readings.

cultural objects, a vocabulary of motives and justifications, a mythology, and so on. The same is true of the large world of hunters and fishermen, of the world of pop music, of motorcycles, of antique collectors, and of all shareable activities available in a society.

None of these cultural worlds is the exclusive domain of a single social group. Barber shops used to be exclusively male hangouts where the symbolic systems of baseball, pool, hunting, and cars were invoked, but the men varied by age, religion, ethnicity, and social class. But insofar as the boundaries of one kind of world are the same as the boundaries for another kind of world, a single group tends to emerge with that uniquely combined culture. To the extent that major social cleavages are congruent with a whole list of communicative worlds, of course, the possibility of communication across the lines of cleavage are lessened, subcultural distinctiveness is enhanced, and conflicts are likely to be acute. A particularly painful example of this may be found in the split between French and "English" Canada. The conflict is exacerbated because the line between Frenchmen and "Englishmen" is congruent with the line between the province of Quebec and the rest of the country, the line between French language use and the use of other languages, the line between a thoroughly Roman Catholic area and dominantly Protestant areas, and to a very considerable degree the line between lower and middle class. The probability of any real integration of French and "English" Canada in the foreseeable future, therefore, is remote.

Communicative barriers (consisting, in turn, of barriers to social interaction) are, ipso facto, cultural barriers. Where the means of transportation and communication are localized, as in developing countries, the result is the familiar regional culture. Ethnic groups may arise for the same social reason; it is possible to erect social barriers just as strong as barriers provided by the expense of travel.

It is also possible for a variety of communication systems to grow up *across* traditional social barriers, even though the vast majority of participants in each camp may not even be aware of their existence. Consider, for example, specialized consumer publications that appeal to hobbyists, active or vicarious; underground presses that quote each other but are never cited by the establishment press; radio frequency bands open only to those with certain skills and special equipment; and the (presumably) underground railway that has supported radical leaders wanted by the police. At the same time, persons with overlapping memberships in contrasting groups provide communication links between apparently isolated sets of individuals. An elderly female may belong to an Audubon society as well as to her church's youth board, while the young male captain of the church-league basketball team may also belong to a cycle club. This is how birdwatchers may come to know some motorcycle jargon and how some understanding across the lines of age and sex is possible.

Cultures, as well as societies, are highly differentiated. This is true of even the relatively "simple" societies we like to think of as fully cohesive, tradition bound, and homogeneous. In fact, the consensus regarding religious matters is far from complete—witness Malinowski's (1948) report of varying beliefs concerning procreation and spirits of the dead within the same society. Each participant in a subculture has a unique perspective based on his unique social position, interests, experiences, and the cultural "worlds" available to him. Thus, members do not participate in exactly the same parts of the subculture.

In consequence, "the member" or "the participant" is not identical with the subculture, and the believer is not identical with the belief system. To be sure, the subculture (in total) is carried by the network of communication in which the total set of members participates and cannot be said to exist apart from that network of interactions, but each individual member's participation is specialized, and most participants devote far less than their full time to the activity, whatever it is. Applying this to belief systems we would insist that the vast majority of believers are in rather substantial ignorance of the fine points of most belief systems in which they participate. Only a handful of specialists has any claim at all to authority regarding the inner logic of the belief system. It may well be that most belief systems cannot possibly be detailed in full by any *one* person.[9]

[9]Converse (1964) demonstrates this rather convincingly.

Thus, culture derives a kind of supraindividual power from its group expression; it *does* consist of something more and greater than what is available to any one individual participant. Culture in general—though it has been reported most clearly and frequently for religion in particular—often produces certain intensely personal experiences involving feelings of reliance on, subordination to, and identification with, a force beyond and outside the individual himself. Durkheim's very definition of collective representations involved constraints which, though external to the individual, must be generated out of the interactions among individuals.[10]

There is a very clear moral here for those who do empirical studies of belief. Interviews will produce partial and sometimes inconsistent descriptions of the belief system. The partiality is natural and entirely to be expected and simply reflects what we have discussed above. The inconsistency may indicate that within the major belief system there are one or more minor variants. Of course, these too are likely to be fully described by no one respondent. The fact that the complete belief system cannot be reconstructed from interviews with a few believers is not evidence that a belief system does not exist. In exactly the same way, the failure of any given number of Shell Oil Company employees to describe the total corporate structure does not mean that Shell Oil does not exist.

All societies are differentiated. The extent of differentiation ranges all the way from that which characterizes folk societies such as the Andaman Islanders to that of enormous urban societies such as the United States and the Soviet Union. Social differentiation is a concomitant of institutional differentiation which consists of the specialization and routinization of activities in general. In relatively undifferentiated societies, a single social structure is used to organize all collective activities that need to be organized: work, religion, art, war, education, and so on. This social structure usually assigns positions to individuals on the basis of age, sex, and descent; the kinship system is the basis for organizing any activity.

As activities develop into specialties, special-purpose structures arise to organize them. A general-purpose organization such as a

[10]See Durkheim (1965:especially Book II, Chapters 6 and 7).

kinship structure is a very clumsy basis for organizing the activities of full-time specialists with abstruse skills. Highly differentiated societies perpetuate certain bodies of knowledge and belief through such generalized structures as families, cliques, public schools, men's clubs, and the mass media. But in addition they also use highly specialized structures not available to all, such as professional associations, theology schools, monasteries, and laboratories. These preserve, develop, and propagate more detailed and specialized knowledge for which the general purpose organization is not suitable.

The extent of institutional differentiation is of first importance as a social condition affecting the culture carried by a society.[11] The greater the institutional differentiation the more likely it is that there will exist a great variety of belief systems. The extent and type of institutional differentiation not only distinguishes "primitive" from "modern" societies, but also points to differences within and among "modern" societies. It is particularly interesting that despite its complexity, the Soviet Union *appears* not to manifest the variety of belief systems one would expect of an urban industrial society. A detailed study, if it were possible, might uncover a considerable network of clandestine belief.

Differing modes of institutionalization in different cultures produce unique characteristics in the social and intellectual life of each society. Two societies with equal institutional differentiation may specialize differently. The manner in which a particular people classify their own ideas and embody that classification in the organization of their activities can be called their mode of institutionalization. Institutions are the established divisions of culture, consisting of norms, values, information, orientations, and so on, which people have standardized and put together as a set of social activities embodied in and implemented and perpetuated by a particular social structure. For example, *we* combine the regulation of sexual activity, the expression of love, and the socialization of children as necessarily connected activities, bound up in a single organization—the family. Yet it is conceivable that these activities could be separated and tied to different social structures such as

[11]For the classic source here, see Durkheim (1947).

houses of prostitution, institutionalized emotional partnerships between successful men and young boys, and collective nursery farms. A well-publicized example of a somewhat different organization of these activities is the kibbutz, in which day-to-day rearing of children is differentiated from their procreation.[12]

These characteristics often determine a people's special abilities and problems. The institutionalization of science in Western culture produces a constant tension and interplay between logic and empirical research, for example, but no connection between empirical truth and traditionalism, beauty, or moral rectitude. The ancient Mayas put mathematics and astronomy together with religion, and technology together with agriculture. This influenced mathematics through the problems that were posed for it, and technology through the efficacy of the available conceptual tools for the solution of problems. Thus the way a people attacks problems and the kinds of problems they attack are responsive to the mode of institutionalization.

SUMMARY. Our approach to the study of flying saucer cults, the ecumenical movement, popular science, individualism, and a host of other interesting problem areas in the sociology of belief *begins with the treatment of belief systems as instances of culture.* As we have seen, such a treatment leads immediately to a set of propositions, empirical generalizations, and further questions on the relationship between ideas on the one hand and social interaction and structure on the other. Many possible traditional questions in the sociology of knowledge and the sociology of religion are taken as answered at the outset by this approach. What is the source of the superpersonal power of a belief? How does a belief relate an individual to a group? How do members of different groups in the same society come to share bits and pieces of each subculture? Such questions, now treated as commonplace characteristics of culture, were taken as things to be explained by writers such as Durkheim whose conclusions provided this, our starting point.

[12]See Spiro (1958) and Rabin (1965).

The Social Contexts of Belief

Belief systems exist in two social contexts which make them intelligible, a context of organization and a context of meaning. Even the context of meaning is social in that it refers to the process of symbolic communication. A central task for the sociology of belief is to relate the characteristics of belief systems to features of the social contexts in which they occur.

THE ORGANIZATIONAL CONTEXT. The organizational context of belief may be divided into two parts, the specific social structure that carries the belief, and the general environment in which these organizational vehicles exist. This general environment consists of the overlapping institutional structures of the society, the networks of communication, the economy and polity, and the demographic structures. This most general environment consists of the basic parameters of the society—the way its members make a living and how they organize their collective life.

This general environment is exterior to the specific organizational vehicles which carry belief and is the environment to which these organizational vehicles must respond. Its effects on belief are profound but indirect. It acts *through* the more highly specialized organizations by changing the conditions of their existence. Thus, the general shift in any given area of the American economy away from a large number of small and highly competitive business organizations toward a relatively smaller number of very large quasi-monopolistic corporations has produced vast changes in the nature of work—in the types of careers available for workers—and hence in the kinds of beliefs about appropriate behavior which are likely to be transmitted by the family.

Social Structures That Carry Beliefs. The countless social structures that carry belief may be divided into two general types for the purpose of discussion. First *associations* are social organizations called into being more or less intentionally for some specific purpose (or purposes). The purpose may or may not be the belief system itself. In the case of churches, it is. In the case of commercial organizations, it probably is not. Second, there are relatively unspecialized social structures, such as a *fellowship* or *brotherhood,* which may have no such clear charter. In fact any social organization, from a town to a matrilineal clan, may carry belief systems that may have nothing to do with what members conceive to be the "purpose" of the organization.

An unspecialized social structure, or general purpose organization such as a kinship structure, a neighborhood, or a peer group, may have no special purpose or organizational charter other than the general well-being of members. Belief systems carried by such general fellowships share certain characteristics imposed on them by their social structure.

1. These belief systems are not systematically developed, there being no band of full-time specialists to perform the tasks of developing or explaining the belief.

2. They tend to deal with general and socially applicable beliefs rather than with esoteric or abstract knowledge.

3. Since interaction tends to be diffuse, beliefs are not presented in isolation from other interests.

4. Personal commitment can be high because diffuse emotional sanctions may be employed during socialization. For example, consider the traditional competitive-sexist belief system carried by an organization no more specialized than "American schoolboys." "Members" are likely to be strongly committed to a competitive, sexist view of interpersonal relations which they think of as being "reality" because in this regard there are sanctions for "proper" behavior in a wide variety of life situations: family, school, peer group, and mass media. Both competitiveness and sexism have traditionally been highly functional for many adult males. As beliefs about what is proper behavior they are not presented as separate from other beliefs, for instance, concerning professional interests. No formal organization exists, however, to develop the dogma of competitiveness and sexism and subject them to rigorous scholarship. They are carried by a loose brotherhood and not clearly separated from other beliefs about other things.

5. Societal consensus is likely to be low on beliefs carried by unspecialized social structures because there is no authoritative organization to legitimately settle differences of belief, despite the sexist example given above on which consensus seems high. In fact, it is a bone of contention. The paradox of low societal consensus associated with beliefs that appear to be unquestioned is explained by the very disorganization of the organizational vehicle. You have to organize even to conflict! Father may know that toads produce warts but he doesn't know why, and who argues with him? To

refuse a beer offered by a certain category of American workingman is to risk becoming involved in a fight. Isolated beliefs that are carried by unspecialized social structures are justified by the response "because" when one asks "why." What we ordinarily call "folk belief" is typically carried by such a fellowship.[1]

Associations are specialized social structures which are at least partly responsible for carrying all systematically developed belief systems. Even the beginnings of theology in folk religions are to be explained by the development of specialized roles and specifically religious associations. By definition, they are the type of organizational vehicle which provides full-time specialists specifically for the task of developing and perpetuating the belief system. At the very least they provide amateurs who devote vast quantities of time and energy to those ends.

Associations provide resources such as money, man-hours, buildings, and social power; they provide jobs (and, in so doing, motivate commitment in a new and powerful way), and they devote resources to ancillary activities. The latter include meeting internal needs (coffee for volunteers, tension release for believers, coordination of effort) as well as performing external services (information clearinghouse, liaison with other institutional structures, public relations). Such services mobilize social power and make the belief system a much more potent voice in human affairs, but they also necessarily involve the belief system in the mundane, often with profound consequences.

Associations are thought of as single-purpose organizations. But since coordinated action is the source of social power, an association that has been constructed for one purpose is potentially useful for many other purposes. The belief system, that is, usually does not impose a unique purpose on general organizational activities such as recruitment, collection of funds, public relations, and so on.

[1]Note that we do not refer to typical folk religion here. The religion of a folk society is usually organized around one or more full-time specialists, though in some such societies the specialist is still required to produce most of his own food. We are referring here to bodies of belief which are typically concerned with secular matters: toads cause warts, don't walk under ladders, breaking mirrors brings seven years of bad luck, and the like.

Organizations can be reused almost as flexibly as buildings. This general utility results in the fact that (in spite of their definition, and indeed their origin) associations tend to exhibit multitudes of purposes if they have been around long enough.

As associations age, they tend to acquire additional purposes or to change their purpose to fit changes in their own membership or in the surrounding society. A striking example of this is the March of Dimes which, when its first goal was achieved, changed its focus from the eradication of infantile paralysis to the eradication of children's diseases. Thus the belief system, even as a raison d'être, undergoes transformation as a consequence of being carried by an association. This is the rule, but there are exceptions. The Women's Christian Temperance Union (WCTU) is an example of an organization which has retained both the major tenets of its belief and the structure of its organization in the face of a changing external environment by the social tactic of recruiting its members from a new segment of society (Gusfield, 1955).

Associations are probably never the *only* organizational vehicle for a belief system. At any one time there may be several different associations, at different stages of institutionalization, carrying portions of a belief system in a given society. More importantly, if the belief system has developed to the point of being carried by an association, it is sure to be carried by unspecialized structures in the society as well. Let us cite the belief system vaguely referred to as the Movement in the late 1960s and the middle 1970s. The Movement is an amalgam composed of the Peace Movement, Women's movements, the new politics movements, and aspects of consumer rights and the other more or less intellectual forms of populism. It is carried by a variety of fairly highly institutionalized formal organizations such as NOW (National Organization of Women), by a host of only slightly institutionalized local peace and women's rights organizations, and by a vehicle composed largely of people in a given type of university setting.

The association generally attempts to acquire exclusive legitimacy in decision-making about or on behalf of the belief system but is seldom fully successful in the attempt. Still, when associations or institutional structures deal with one another (as in the continuing debate between science and religion) they *must* treat one another as spokesmen for the respective belief systems; a largely unorganized public may provide neither a clear or legitimate spokesman nor a target. An example can be found in the quite typical development of movements of the Left. Great movements of reform invariably involve squabbling between associations. The American civil rights movement, the Russian Revolution, and the Protestant Reformation were characterized by such bitter competition for exclusive franchise among associations that for long periods the general goals were subordinated to a struggle for power between agencies.

Among associations that carry belief systems, it is worth distinguishing between those in which perpetuating the belief system *is* the organizational charter such as churches and graduate schools, and those in which the charter includes other activities for which the belief system is a means, such as corporations and hospitals. The theoretical importance of this distinction stems from the application of performance criteria: the first type of association will evaluate its own successes primarily in terms of membership, social power, and status among peers, but the second will evaluate itself in terms of its social action product—the successful application of the beliefs. The behavior of the organization in relation to the belief system will be correspondingly different. Let us call an association for which the raison d'être consists only of the development and perpetuation of the belief system as an intrinsic value a *cult,* and an association for which the belief system is a means rather than an end a *concern.*

Few associations, of course, are pure cult or pure concern. After the organization is broken up into different parts which behave as if they had different purposes, associations may be internally differentiated and a concern may have a cult as a differentiated part, such as a committee on party goals established by a national political party or a committee on traditions within a large fraternal organization. Party members usually expect the committee to serve the goals of the party, but committee members are apt to see the party as implementing goals specified by the committee.

Concerns, that is, take a pragmatic approach to the belief systems they carry, while cults are inclined to treat them as sacred. In consequence, the belief system carried by a concern is apt to be much more socially useful, but also much more intimately tied to a particular historical circumstance. This contrasting stance toward the concrete actuality versus the abstract ideal affects the role of the concern or the cult in revolution and social control. The cult responds to the inner logic of the belief system without much reference to its practical consequences and is likely to be extremely conservative in terms of adopting *changes* which have originated in its constituency. From the point of view of this constituency, however, it is likely to be radical in some respects because its specific charter to follow its own drummer *may* lead it in directions not popular in the practical world. The concern, on the other hand, responds to pressures in the environment and is likely to be willing to compromise principle to accomplish practical goals. The concern is likely to be conservative vis-à-vis the logical development of the belief system and to hold on tenaciously to the past while it is radical in its willingness to try new approaches on a purely technological level. The cult and the concern are almost by definition in conflict with each other.

As an example of the difference between cult and concern, consider the large university dominated by a graduate school and the ethos of publish (more) or perish, and a two-year community college nearby. The town/gown conflict arises in part because in the university the charter is to follow the logic of the belief system and this may lead to behavior that seems weird to townsmen (ignoring niceties of dress and mannerism), radical to state legislators (analyzing popular mythologies about society), and is conservative (ignoring input from student culture). The community college is likely to seem more "down to earth" (like high school teachers) to townsmen, more safe (supporting popular mythologies) to state legislators, and be less conservative in taking on innovations in teaching (using tomorrow's teaching methods to put across the academic knowledge of 20 years ago).

In many respects the conflict between the upper bureaucracy of the Roman Catholic Church and its lower priesthood is a clash between cult and concern.

The discussion above might be summarized in the general proposition that to the degree the organizational vehicle that carries a belief system is dominated by a *cult*, the belief system will remain "pure" but will face problems of retaining its relevance to some community of believers. To the extent an organizational vehicle is dominated by a *concern*, the belief system may remain relevant to a community of believers but it is likely to change rapidly and become highly compromised.

Elements of Associations. Associations can be described structurally in terms relevant to their belief-carrying capacities. This classification can be viewed equally well from either of two perspectives; it is at the same time a list of organizational parts and of types of participation, depending on whether the reader's perspective is that of the organization or the members. Associations are composed of a *corporate body* which includes the leadership, all specialized roles, and employees, and a *membership* consisting of all formal members who do not currently occupy specialized roles. The corporate body, of course, may be internally very complex or it may be small and simple. Membership implies no more than formal affiliation (though members may be active participants as well). Formal affiliation is important as a declaration of identification and as a potential inclusion in a communication network. Both the membership and the corporate body are part of a potentially much larger social category, the *community of believers,* which also includes participants in the belief system who do not affiliate themselves with the association, although they may act in concert with it in practice.

An association in which the corporate body is a large proportion of the membership, or in which the membership is a large proportion of the community of believers, is said to be highly *mobilized* in that it is prepared to take immediate full-scale action close to the limit of its potential. The typical new cult is an organizational anomaly to politicians or officers in institutional structures because of its lack of mobilization. Initially, it is so weak as to be negligible, even though the community of believers may be very large. Because persons within it pay selective attention to associations relevant to their beliefs, any cult is potentially a major power; if it can mobilize the community it may become an enormous and effective organization (for example, the John Birch Society affects the whole conservative front).

The Degree of Institutionalization. One of the fundamental problems of social organization is the fact that in order to accomplish a task effectively and repeatedly over a long period of time resources and effort must be channeled away from the accomplishment of the task itself and toward the construction and maintenance of the organization which is to accomplish the task.[2] It is also necessary to set up some sort of working arrangement with other organized activities in the same society to avoid conflict and to prevent opposition from arising and becoming organized. Some organizations, as a tenet of belief, refuse to divert significant proportions of their resources for these purposes, thereby determining their organizational form and setting limits on what they can accomplish. In refusing to pay the cost, they abandon the benefits of solving the two general kinds of organizational problems: internal problems, including coordination, authority, tension management, division of labor, ancillary services, and so on; and external problems, including public relations, liaison with other organizations, access to sources of societal power, and so on.[3] Other organizations, notably those associated with business and government, hasten to establish organizational machinery and in so doing become large, stable, and compromised. They trade organizational solidity for purity of belief. The extent to which an association does pay the cost and reap the consequences can be called the degree of institutionalization.

Internal and external organizational solutions are mutually rele-

[2]See King (1956), Selznick (1960), and Clark (1948).

[3]This seems to be true of the New Left. See Dolbeare (1971).

vant. An organization with the power to affect the social environment is useful for purposes other than those specified in the abstract belief system and therefore comes to be used by members and nonmembers alike to attain a variety of social goals. Power constitutes a stake in the existing system and it is enhanced through compromise. Making external alliances is facilitated by internal policies; isolation and hostility to the external world give way to cooptation and cooperation as dominating strategies. The fact that making an internal organizational decision entails making an external one, and vice versa, is one of the reasons for the organizational dilemma: The power to implement a belief is bought at the price of compromise of the belief itself.[4]

[4]The major apparent exception to this rule is the government of the People's Republic of China which appears to have become progressively *less* conciliatory to old ways as it has become more powerful and more securely entrenched. Other revolutionary governments have followed this same path, however, only to eventually succumb. Whether China will remain an exception is only answerable in the future. The whole literature in this area suggests that it will not.

The sequence should be as follows if China is to follow the usual script. The death of Mao will trigger a power struggle that will end with the dominance of professional bureaucrats. With the government of professionals will come a deemphasis on purity of belief and a deemphasis of the radical democratization of the Mao era. With the deemphasis of belief and democratization will come the reestablishment of systems of rank and privilege. Verbal commitment to revolutionary struggle and equality will probably continue. As they fade in practice, ceremonies celebrating them may increase. Social control is likely to weaken in the long run and it is probable that the sheer amount of individual testifying will not only decrease but come to be regarded as old fashioned and slightly embarrassing. It would be a mistake to expect China to become basically similar to the United States or Europe, however. It is likely that internal schism will follow the beginning of the reign of bureaucrats. In the long run, the social gap between workers, peasants, and soldiers on one hand and the bureaucrats (and their children) should become as great or perhaps greater as it is in the other industrialized nations, protestations to the contrary notwithstanding.

A second and more difficult exception is Nazi Germany which did not become more conciliatory as it became established and, in fact, became more intransigent with reference to the Jewish question. It should be kept in mind, however, that the Nazi movement was only in power for 13 years; how it might have behaved later with reference to "inferior races" (at least those outside its borders) had the war ended in a stalemate is unknown.

The process of institutionalization described in this chapter does not occur at uniform speed in all cases. Many groups hang on to their sectarian fervor, or some part of it, for a very long while. Others capitulate before there is a real threat.

First, uncompromising associations are, of necessity, relatively *small.*[5] Otherwise the problems of coordination alone would be overwhelming. Since the number of members generally has reference to contributions as well as to the base for political support, such groups are usually poor and relatively powerless. Small size is what permits interaction to be personal and face-to-face, and it does not force the relationships to be functionally specific. In short, the fabric of social interaction in the group (rather than merely interaction in subgroups or at coffee time) may consist of primary relationships—a teacher and his or her disciples, for instance. Small size does not permit extensive role differentiation so that such groups have a simple division of labor and may exhibit great consensus. These factors predispose members to a high level of personal involvement.[6]

Second, such associations are *highly mobilized.* Lacking institutional structure, they may capture the imaginations of a few people for a long time or of many people briefly, but they are not equipped to sustain the interest and activity of large numbers over a long time. As noted above, however, they can command a much higher proportion of what each member has to devote than a larger and less task-oriented group. What such groups can accomplish unaided is relatively predictable; it is what they are accomplishing right now. Lack of external arrangements makes it difficult for them to solicit aid. They tend to fall apart completely for lack of social facilitation when they are not operating at peak effort: The task *is* what organizes the membership.

Third, their existence is *precarious.* This follows from high mobilization, lack of external support and power, and lack of internal organization. They depend heavily on the health and approval of a few members; anything that goes wrong can spell disaster. They are very much at the mercy of giant organizations in

[5]There is reputed to be a religious organization known as the Cooneyites in the United States and the 2 x 2s in Canada which rejects organization entirely but manages some kind of continuity. There is no literature on this group. They would certainly be the extreme case.

[6]An extended discussion of this type of grouping may be found in Wach (1944).

the same institutional area which collectively set the life conditions for competitors. Uncompromising associations tend to spring up and die like weeds. The arrangements for recruitment and socialization of new members are so rudimentary that turnover is a severe problem for such a group. Group dissolution is so frequent, however, that the present membership of such a group is usually composed of people who have previously belonged to several others of the same organizational type (Lofland, 1966). Examples of such groups would include new political parties, fraternal organizations, and small, highly deviant religious organizations.

These considerations apply to concerns as well as to cults (consider the life circumstances of small business, for example). Yet the effect of the degree of institutionalization on the belief system of a concern is a much simpler problem. The belief system of a concern must adapt to the existing social environment because the goal of a concern is action in this environment. Large and powerful concerns can often do this by changing the social environment, but the small and mobilized concern cannot, and hence must adapt to it or disappear. Thus the belief system of a small concern rather than reflecting the effects of its own logic really reflects the effects of the social conditions under which it is trying to accomplish its goal. It is the most pliable type of social vehicle.

The cult experiences much less pressure from the nature of the task because the task is not in the outside world, but has to do with development of the belief system itself.

Among associations that do not subordinate preservation of the belief system to other aspects of the charter, religious associations have been most thoroughly studied. The names we use—sect for a small and uncompromising group and institutional church for the organizationally more developed association—reflect our reliance on this type of study. Historically, the church-sect typology has been developed on the basis of several different theoretical interests: denominationalism, schism, doctrinal purity, type of internal organization, type of belief, role in doctrinal conservatism or change, social policies, and characteristics of the membership. Because these phenomena are all causally related, the theoretical interests converge: wherever you begin, you are led to all the others.[7]

This is a type of causal cycle through time. Selection of an alternative belief has organizational implications that set the conditions of life for the belief system. That selection of an organizational alternative has implications for belief which, in turn, will have future organizational significance, and so on. Analysis could begin equally well with any of the elements; a stance adopted in relation to one of them has implications for all the others.

Let us illustrate by beginning with belief. The basic dilemma is the fact that to the extent beliefs are to be implemented in the larger society, they are affected by the means used to implement them. Substantive beliefs themselves reflect solutions to internal and external organizational problems. To avoid the necessary doctrinal compromises that follow from these solutions, it is necessary to follow the organizational strategy of the most extreme sect and therefore opt for a precarious existence at best. In a growing cult, problems of coordination alone provide strong pressures for devotion of resources to internal organization. To escape these pressures (as well as to remain small), groups often fragment along doctrinal lines. To avoid the corrupting influence of worldly affairs, cult members typically enforce some kind of encapsulation on themselves, either physical isolation (such as communal living), social isolation (prohibitions on specified types of social intercourse), or cultural insulation (idiosyncratic dress, food, and behavior).

If we extend the theory regarding the institutionalized church to nonreligious organizations, relatively institutionalized cults should show the following organizational characteristics:

1. *Societal value of organization.* An association with enough wealth and power to accomplish something will tend to be used for purposes other than those specified in its charter. The association becomes a target of social protest movements as well as a cat's-paw for vested interests, whether its members like it or not. In the last

[7]Yinger (1970:especially 251-281). Let us make a general reference to the sect-church literature here. Yinger (1970:224-281) provides a discussion and an elaborate bibliography.

half century, for example, churches have been forced to respond to the demand that they provide personal adjustment, mental health, satisfactory marriages, intellectual stimulation, recreation, community services, arbitration, law and order, welfare, comfort to high school football teams, and Rotary speakers, while supplying moral leadership to reactionaries and revolutionaries alike in their spare time. Accepting these burdens, of course, helped maintain the power of churches in mundane affairs when that power was threatened. Similarly, universities attempted to gain temporal power by providing services from management clinics to gardening consultation, only to be held responsible by the student bodies for social ills from poverty to war.

2. *Connections with other institutions.* Power involves an association in the complexity of societal organization. Gaining clout at the polls inevitably results in coordination with political parties. The priest must watch what he says on Sunday because some governor may actually *do* it. Professors cannot play intellectual games without being called to testify before the Supreme Court or to advise the Pentagon. Where a sect can take an extreme stand on an issue ignoring all its practical ramifications, a church finds its pronouncements as well as its organizational affairs enmeshed in the tangle of societal collective action. This is not merely a corollary of power (as envy is a corollary of prestige); it is the fact that the ability to execute a program, even in part, subjects the person or organization to the entire range of consequences of the program.

Gaining societal power also entails preventing opposition from crystallizing. This is accomplished by taking all other interests into consideration and by not offending anyone unless absolutely necessary. To be able to do this an association not only needs full-time personnel, it also needs a great deal of firsthand information concerning the goals and operating strategies of other organizations. The institutional structure of a complex society includes a great deal of liaison. Schools cooperate with churches, political parties cooperate with unions, fraternal orders cooperate with basketball leagues, and so on.

3. *Professional Careers.* Church-type associations are able to

develop elaborate belief systems, to organize large memberships, and to relate to other institutions because they have full-time professional members who devote their lives to a sequence of offices in the association. To the people who depend upon it for their livelihood, the existence of careers makes the association valuable as a thing in itself, entirely apart from its goals. Career commitment is a new type of member commitment which is unique in being stronger than usual but less goal-directed. Rather than being commitment to a belief, it is commitment to an association. This kind of commitment is inherently conservative because in a situation of choice the more valued entity, the organization, will be preserved and the less valued entity, the belief, will be abandoned. Associations that have reached the stage in which career-type members are dominant have lost their ability to be radical. Earlier stages of association are dominated by persons whose commitment is primarily to the belief system and only secondarily to the organization.

Vesting the right to make legitimate interpretations of doctrine in an office instead of an individual or a principle has further implications. Provisions must be made for selecting the proper, but uninspired, official. Technical complexities tend to absorb time and interest at the expense of simple eternal verities. Professional jealousies and jurisdictional disputes arise.

4. *Internal Differentiation.* The corporate body is distinct from the rest of the membership, and develops its own goals and procedures. A current example of this process as a source of strain in an association is the widening gap in belief separating the Protestant clergy from Protestant congregations.

The membership itself is heterogeneous in terms of belief, other social characteristics, and level of activity. Consensus is relatively low in this type of cult, but then its organization facilitates containment of conflicts based on disagreement. Interaction (except in subgroups or in special circumstances such as coffee hour) is less apt to be primary, and therefore only differences fundamental to belief need to be considered, and even those are not compounded by personal affect.

A small portion of the membership fills a set of part-time roles in the corporate body; this portion of the membership is extremely active and devoted and (though socially closer to the professional portion of the corporate body) tends to represent the membership by being goal oriented and unsophisticated in doctrine. A much larger proportion of the membership (though usually not more than half) maintains the level of activity formally requested of all (attending most meetings, for example) while a large proportion of the membership shades off in activity from not very much to none whatever. This structure gives the association the *potential* for action that accompanies low mobilization but unfortunately tends to give it a lack of urgency or excitement at the same time.[8]

5. *Societal Status of Membership.* For all the reasons listed above, the membership of the institutionalized church, and especially of the most active membership group, tends to be drawn from that portion of the population with active participation and some stake in the status quo. Sect members tend to be the societal nonparticipants, the dropouts and dispossessed, but joining and participating in a church-type association is a primary means for establishing personal connection with the institutional structure of the society. Therefore the representation of higher statuses in the population is exaggerated, and while *all* statuses are represented, the lower status members represent the *respectable* segment of their class.[9]

Institutionalization and Belief. The belief system carried by a highly institutionalized cult is very likely to be different from that carried by a less institutionalized cult for the reasons we have outlined above. It is likely to be at least superficially systematic because a staff of specialists for exegesis is available. The higher degree of system may very well have been produced after the fact by a team of apologists but it is likely to be there nonetheless.

[8]Consider, for example, the volunteers who go from door to door on behalf of communitywide or national philanthropic associations.

[9]On social status and religious participation see Yinger (1970:282-309).

The level of commitment of members is likely to vary from one extreme to the other within a highly institutionalized cult. Institutionalization is a process in which a few clear, simple, and unambiguous goals become complex, diffuse, and compromised.

More highly institutionalized cults tend to see other societal goals as compatible with their own, to justify the existing order, and to favor slow evolutionary change. Less institutionalized groups tend to view other societal goals with hostility, to attack the existing order, and to favor and expect revolutionary change. More highly institutionalized cults are likely to favor compromise and accommodation rather than polarization and destruction.

Besides favoring the status quo (or at least accepting it as given), the highly institutionalized cult is conservative in another sense. The organization and the institutional context are seen as too valuable to be thrown away for matters of principle. Risky alternatives, for either the cult or the society, are not chosen by career officers or by members who have something to lose. No simple or extreme position is taken partly by way of covering all bets, partly because of the heterogeneity of the membership, and partly because consideration must be given to who might be offended by an action and how many organizational resources must be devoted to mollifying him. On the other hand, extreme positions are natural outcomes of the structure of the uninstitutionalized cult where polarization of issues provides simplicity and where intense interaction under conditions of isolation makes for extreme and idiosyncratic perspectives.

The time perspective of the highly institutionalized group is *sub specie aeternitatis,* whereas the uninstitutionalized group is limited to the here and now in its beliefs, just as its organization, through failure to provide for membership turnover resulting from birth and death, is limited to the present generation of believers. Solutions *must* be radical and immediate because the group has no yesterday, no tomorrow, no day after tomorrow.

In summary, the belief systems associated with uninstitutionalized cults involve faith that a single, simple solution (or grandiose avoidance of the problem) will immediately solve everything.

Highly institutionalized cults have faith that in the long run, no matter how bad things look, slow amelioration will improve some things, but no simple, certain, or immediate means to total salvation is expected. The contrast is between emotional zeal and patient wisdom.[10]

The history of the Salvation Army in Canada provides an excellent example of the institutionalization process and its consequences. Originating in Britain as the result of schism within Methodism, the Salvation Army was first established in Canada in 1883. The new sect came into an environment characterized by urban growth and increasing separation of the established churches from the urban masses. Methodism, which itself had originated in a sectarian schism earlier in the century, had become established, socially powerful, heavily invested in religious edifices, and composed of trained, professional ministers and well-to-do "respectable" members. It had little appeal and little relevance to the new urban masses. The Army adopted colorful evangelical strategies, ministering with the fervor of the sect to the drunk on the street and the prostitute in the brothel. It recruited from among those to whom it ministered and, in the manner of sects organized along military lines, took its workers in as lifetime employees.

The practical work by Army members on the street led to dramatic successes among individuals and to increasing power and acceptance for the organization. As the Army succeeded, it backed away from its exclusive emphasis on evangelism and began investing more of its resources in building a stable organization. This produced disaffection and desertion of some workers, and also forced the organization to abandon its efforts in areas of little

[10]See Yinger (1970:251-281), Troeltsch (1931), Gerth and Mills (1958:especially 267-285), Demerath and Hammond (1969:157-163), Brinton (1965), and King (1956). Although what we have described here is similar to the so called sect-to-church process, we have deliberately avoided using the language of the sociology of religion for reasons mentioned in Chapter 2. Basically, we feel that there are a number of important sociological dimensions along which "church" and "sect" differ, that these dimensions are not invariably related, and that they do not all follow automatically from the dilemma of worldly power. Furthermore, we regard this statement as applicable to a whole range of organizations and beliefs, not just explicitly religious ones.

support and concentrate on areas in which it was finding greater support.

As increasing attention was paid to the mechanics of organization, a correspondingly smaller amount of attention was paid to personal street-corner evangelism. Schism appeared between the leaders, who were by now concerned with organizational solidity, and the evangelists, who were concerned with the Word not with the buildings. (This is the point at which purity of belief is typically traded for organizational longevity.) A further change took place during the shift from evangelism to organization: the workers, who had typically been recruited from among down-and-outs, were replaced by professionally trained persons of relatively high social status. Training schools were established and the passing of the old-time Salvationist was complete.

This major shift of focus from religiously charged street-corner evangelism to bureaucratically organized social welfare took about 30 years. The Army has since become even more established and more linked with other institutions in the community. It is also more challenged by other new movements filled with the fire of uncompromised belief.[11]

THE CONTEXT OF MEANING. The shared orientations on which social life is based provide a meaningful context in which seemingly cryptic messages may be understood. A person rarely needs to say more than a small part of what he or she means; the rest is implicit. One person's ability to understand another is due to his ability to place the other's statements within some *context of meaning,* some mutually understood set of definitions. Meaning inheres in statements, to be sure, but language seems less rich than the things it is asked to express and frequently enough one must understand a whole context of meaning in order to understand a simple declaration. We are confronted every day by a myriad of statements which involve some claim to be true. Some of them are so simple and direct that we simply accept them without thinking.

[11]See Clark (1948) for a history of the Salvation Army in Canada.

Some are so complex and involuted that only the person who made them can understand them. Some of the statements that are so simple and direct that we accept them without thinking involve highly local language, symbolism, and allegory that make them totally senseless to an outsider. Do you remember your first experience trying to learn the idioms of another language? *Il n'y a pas de quoi*, for instance.

A brief descriptive statement, such as "there is a cat," is the most simple of these statements. If the grammar is understood and there is some consensus on whether the noun "cat" refers to a feline or to a man, the content of the statement is not a real problem. But in the analysis of most beliefs and belief systems things are not this simple. The referent of the noun may not be easily understood; the noun may be a short-cut reference to a very long and complex statement about which there is less than full consensus. Try "there is a Christian," for example.

The statements we encounter daily run from such simple descriptive sentences as "there is a cat" to incredibly complex belief systems in which there are many private or "in" meanings to be unraveled. Studying beliefs and belief systems, one is continually struck by the fact that their depictions of reality are seldom direct interpretations of sense data, as in "there is a cat." Nor are they sense data modified by some evaluative considerations, as in "I am happy at my work." Nor are they sense data and evaluative considerations set in some historical or social context, as in "I oppose further hunting of whales because of their increasing scarcity." They are frequently more like allegory and metaphor, as in "the last shall be first," "I accept Jesus Christ as my personal Savior," and "all power to the people." We have picked dramatic examples here, but many very prosaic beliefs have the same character: "if you want to play on the team you have to obey the rules," "publish or perish," "there's nothing I can do, my hands are tied," or a spectacular example from a British movie of the 1960s, "I'm all right, Jack." Proverbs also have this character: "as ye sow, so shall ye reap," "a priest's stomach is never full."

This allegorical or metaphorical character that makes the substantive content of beliefs so frustrating exists because beliefs are shortcut or *compressed* statements that are highly *conventional.* That is, they compress a large number of images into a few words. At the extreme of compression is the visual image or symbolic object in which a whole battery of already compressed verbal beliefs are still further compressed into one physical object, such as a crucifix or a flag.[12]

By *conventional* we mean that these compressed statements become institutionalized or traditional. They become subject to a high degree of acceptance over a long period of time. They are not idiosyncratic perceptions, such as one has when one feels a pebble through the sole of a thin shoe, but historically developed and richly elaborated, socially shared statements that encapsulate an area of experience. Indeed, the interpretation is so difficult because the belief *becomes* the experience, and other words disappear or do not develop. "I accept the Lord Jesus Christ as my personal Savior," for instance, is a compression of the whole salvation and conversion experience in a fundamentalist Protestant setting. It is highly conventionalized, as is all the language of religious conversion, and extremely compressed.

Much of the above can be summarized in two propositions: (1) To understand a belief it is necessary to place it in a context of meaning because beliefs are compressed. (2) As compression increases, "face validity" (what is interpretable apart from the context) decreases, and a visual or auditory symbol is the ultimate in compression. We are leading to the general premise underlying these two statements, namely that the ultimate context of meaning is the social process of symbolic communication itself.

To communicate and, therefore, to allow a belief system to remain "alive," one must orient his listener not only to the message but also to the type of discourse which is intended. If we say diamonds are hard, you may take the statement literally and attempt to verify it by scratching other materials. If we say that diamonds are

[12]Smelser (1963) has noted the shortcut character of beliefs in another context and developed a rather elaborate model of collective behavior in which "generalized belief systems" play an important part.

beautiful, you understand that quite a different criterion of truth is involved and that the scratch test is completely irrelevant. In fact, the scratch test would have been irrelevant in the first place if we had meant "hard" in the sense that rock music can be "hard." To a burglar, the statement "diamonds are hard" might not only refer to difficulty but might be taken as a statement of life goals equivalent to a merchant's "you get what you pay for." In fact, a statement of belief may mean simply that the speaker wishes to identify himself with a particular group or their announced goals.

The fact that statements of belief are often ambiguous and/or obscure because the meaningful context is not made explicit is not merely an analytic inconvenience, it is an essential characteristic of socially maintained systems of meaning. The statements that explain how a belief system should be understood are seldom part of the public domain; rather, they are contained within the belief system itself. Many folk beliefs are so simple that they can be understood by anyone with a reasonable grasp of the language—"break a mirror and have seven years of bad luck," for example. Occult beliefs, on the other hand, have contexts of meaning so complex and so hidden that only a specialist can unravel a given statement. To a very considerable degree this is also true in science, although probably for different reasons.

A theoretical description of a system of belief, then, must be a construct of the social scientist's, just as in practice it is a construct on the part of humans attempting to communicate.[13] The process of social communication follows this general sequence: Alter addresses a statement to Ego, often a proposal for group action. To understand it, Ego makes a guess (formulates a construct) as to the meaningful context, usually through the imaginative process called "taking the role of the other," and responds with an expression of agreement or disagreement or, if still confused, with a request for further orientation. Reasoning from the response, Alter may per-

[13]The argument that follows this note is not developed in detail. It is drawn from a number of sources generally described as "symbolic interactionist" (See specifically Blumer, 1962). The specific sequence described is based on Bales (1950) who is *not* to be described as a symbolic interactionist. See also Cardwell, 1971:especially 92-94.

ceive, through the same process of role taking, that Ego's construct missed his intended context of meaning in some important respect and return with a statement of orientation. Ego revises his construct, provides a new response, and so on. When both are satisfied that their orientations are sufficiently congruent they agree on an action and then symbolically repair their social relationship, which may have been strained in the interaction. Such constructs do not need to be perfectly accurate but only sufficiently accurate to permit communication and action.

In treating closed systems of meaning as constructs, the sociologist of belief comes to terms with another methodological problem common to all social science and based on the nature of social behavior. The abstract *ideal* system of belief is not identical with the concrete *actual* descripion of behavior. Everyone knows, for example, not only what the law is supposed to be but also that it differs in actual application.

This ability of humans to abstract and to idealize is a precondition for the existence of belief systems and one of the sources of the influence of belief in human events. As actually used by humans, beliefs relate to actual events and the particular social circumstances under which they occur as well as to the realm of the ideal and the absolutely general. For example, an anthropologist may be able to elicit both a consistent account of how the kinship system is supposed to operate and an accurate list of marriages and kin relations from a given informant, and the two need not correspond literally. Indeed, if ideal types were merely inductive generalizations they would have no intrinsic predictive power of their own and would seem to be an unnecessary pedantry.

Belief systems do have their own inner logics and their own set of statements about how things ideally are. Yet, if beliefs are to have social significance they must come to terms with realities that are often far removed from the ideal. Humans are accustomed to this difficulty and behave simultaneously in terms of both the ideal and the real. Witness the uncomfortable interactions between the ideal of democratic politics and the operation of a national convention, or the interaction between Christian theology and the operation of a church bureaucracy. If you criticize an *American Sociological Review* article on race and intelligence, for example, we will justify it as a proximate attempt to meet the abstract goals of science and will meet your specific criticism with the pure logic of scientific method. If you attribute the author's conclusions to personal bias, we will point to the things he has done that, in principle, minimize bias. On the other hand, we recognize the distance between the ideal and the actual and will hasten to note that the author is affiliated with a large urban university faculty noted for its contributions to radical politics. We understand the meaning of the article in the context of both the ideal abstract institutions of science and the specific social circumstances surrounding the research in question. In so doing, we apply two different sets of standards and two different conceptions of cause and effect.

At the ideal level, a belief system can be understood and discussed only in terms of itself; it sets its own context, without which it is not comprehensible. In principle, it is illegitimate to criticize the abstract ideal of a belief system according to any criteria but its own. An hypothesis is true or false without reference to its origin ($E = MC^2$ is not less or more descriptive of reality if accidentally typed by a monkey), and a set of beliefs sets the standards by which they must be understood.[14] However, because of the problems in human communication noted above and because belief systems contain powerful elements of metaphor, the connection between the ideal (the inner logic of the belief system) and the real may be extremely difficult to fathom. In actual social life the connection is made by a speech writer or by an apologist, as required. When no such specialist is available the responsibility falls on the sociologist and the connection must be an invention of his own. A simple example should clarify much of the above. From 1965 until the effort seemed to become hopeless in about 1970, a great deal of effort was invested by apologists to demonstrate that

[14]The argument here concerns the genetic fallacy—the dogma that the origins of a proposition are in no way related to its truth or falsity. For a discussion of the relevance of the social character of knowledge to the application of this rule, see Mannheim (1936:271-274,281-283,292-306).

the actual behavior of the United States in Southeast Asia flowed directly from ideal American values. The amount of energy invested was considerable because the task was difficult. Indeed, it appears to have been impossible.

In the detailed description of belief systems the abstract ideal should be thought of as parallel, point for point, to one or more concrete expressions of the belief system. For example, one might list the ideal values (goals) of science. At the same time, one should call attention to the actual values (goals) of the administrative wing, Cytology Division, Biological Warfare Field Station, in Smallpox, Utah. Science might be defended by saying that warfare is not a scientific value, but it should be added that warfare is a scientific value for *those* scientists and that science does not exist apart from *some* scientists. Thus the abstract ideal is often used as a practical *excuse* for a parallel system of concrete belief that is quite different. The sociologist's concern is that the operation of belief systems in social behavior, such as the interaction patterns within the laboratory mentioned, involve orientation to both abstract and concrete sets of goals and values at the same time. The sociologist of belief must be able to think of a belief system in terms of its own abstract ideal and also to recognize its qualified embodiment in actual social relations.

SUMMARY. The first step in the study of the reciprocal influences of belief and society was to outline the implications of the cultural nature of belief systems. The second step, taken in this chapter, was to take note of the global and often indirect influences that follow from the fact that belief systems exist and are rendered intelligible by the social contexts within which they occur. These include not only the society and numerous smaller social organizations but also the very process of social communication.

5.

The Social Bases of Commitment

Belief systems face two critical problems in the real world, the problem of commitment and the problem of validation. Belief systems persist because they and/or the social vehicles that carry them are able to generate and maintain commitment. For commitment to be maintained, however, a belief system must also, independently, seem to be valid. Commitment and validation are two separate (though mutually relevant) phenomena, in spite of the near universal myth that we are committed *because* our beliefs are valid.

Beliefs must not only seem external and valid, but also worth whatever discomforts believing entails. We often take the trouble to validate our beliefs *because* we are committed to them. The social bases of commitment are discussed in this chapter; the validation of belief systems is discussed in Chapter 6.

Individual commitment may be considered either as a problem in psychology or a problem in sociology. If we see it as a problem in psychology, relevant questions are: What is it about the mental construction of humans that permits them to devote themselves to ideas? What are the personality dynamics of commitment? Why are some persons more accessible to group pressures than others? What congruence may be found between types of personality and types of belief? We leave these questions to be answered by social psychologists.

The sociological problem is to show how groups regularly use human responses to social sanctions in order to produce the phenomena of culture in general and commitment to belief systems in particular. According to what principles are shared systems of beliefs selected or abandoned? What social processes regularly produce commitment in humans? Regardless of the mechanism which translates a social event into a psychological reinforcement in the experience of an individual, how are sanctions socially manipulated so as to produce commitment? In short, *why* does a given group adopt a belief system, and *how* does it produce personal commitment among its members?

GROUP SELECTION OF BELIEFS. Analytically, the selection of beliefs is group reinforcement based on the perceived utility of a belief system for its believers, and the fact that the alternatives to a given belief system may be severely limited if not altogether absent.[1] The two bases exist separately only on paper, however. In real life, a belief system with high utility limits available alternative

[1]See Bandura (1969:261-267). The basis of much of the argument of this chapter and the next is Durkheim's (1965) discussion of the creation of abstract categories of mind and the process in which men come to view "truth" as different from immediate sense data. See specifically pp. 165-182, 216-234, and 484-496.

beliefs by excluding them, and limitation of alternatives increases the utility of whatever one has left. If one must drive nails and has both a hammer and a large stone, the hammer is likely to be chosen. Unless, of course, it has been stolen.

Needless to say, utility for a group is not always identical to individual utility, and it is group utility that motivates group reinforcement. Insofar as humans must collaborate to attain goals, they must compromise with collective utilities. Like it or not, that is, an individual may be committed to a belief by a necessity facing a group to which he belongs.

Let us make it quite clear, however, that beliefs are not called into existence by their utility to some population. It is exactly this kind of mystic functionalism that we are at some pains to avoid. The fact that Christianity had relatively greater penetration into China and Oceania than Confucianism had into the United States and Britain in the nineteenth century is better explained by gunboats than by comparative social "needs" or "functional problems." We are simply arguing that groups retain or change belief systems, as they do other parts of culture, according to the history of reinforcement.

How does one explain why the office workers of the maintenance division of a particular university keep a supply of open-end wrenches on the counter of the front office? Let us consider three types of explanations that might be valid either singly or in combination. First, the wrenches may have intrinsic value. For example, they may be things of beauty to former mechanics who have been "kicked upstairs" to office work. Second, they may have extrinsic value—they are useful for one or more purposes known or unknown to the office workers. Third, the office has a history, and it may be that the present office force was broken in with the wrenches present and no one has yet had the motivation or the authority to remove them.[2]

There is no obvious difficulty in applying intrinsic value or history as explanations of belief, but relating the characteristics of a belief

[2]Note that beliefs are always observed at a particular time, while general theory concerns itself with long-term considerations. Any on-going process, observed at a point in time, will contain some features that appear to contradict its "outcome."

to its utility for a purpose has traditionally posed problems. In principle, however, these problems are not more thorny than in the explanation of the continued presence of open-end wrenches. We must assume that the office force collectively responds to problems regularly brought to the counter by members of the university community. A frequent problem, and one that can be solved easily with little expenditure of energy, is that the bolts used to adjust office swivel chairs are always coming loose. As professors swarm into the office complaining about their chairs (possibly by way of relief from intellectual problems), it is much easier to point to a wrench than it is to fill out the requisition for a work order. Besides, the mechanics find this a demeaning job. The professor says thanks because the wrench is there; if he had to fill out a work order and wait two weeks he would be angry.

But why an open-end wrench? Bolts can be tightened with pliers, scissors held by the points, staplers, two flat ball-point pens, and so on. A bolt *can* be tightened a number of ways, but a wrench has characteristics (possibly because it was designed for the purpose) that makes it especially effective and easy to use: rigidity, fit to the bolt head, and leverage. Frustration is minimized by using the correct tool. That the wrench also has characteristics irrelevant to this use (such as color, trademark, and weight) does not detract from its utility.

Wrenches also have uses other than tightening bolts. As each new professor sweeps into the office, he brings a breeze that tends to blow papers off the counter. The papers *could* be kept in order by filing them immediately, securing them under eighteenth century glass paperweights, keeping clipboards on the counter, and so on. In fact, the wrenches, being the right weight, are used for this purpose, and it matters not whether they were put there "for that purpose."

Thus the characteristics of wrenches, in and of themselves, do not *determine* their use. Yet in explaining why the wrenches are on the counter, the utility of given characteristics of the wrench for this or that use is highly *relevant*. In the hypothetical example, the presence of the wrenches cannot be explained historically because the history is lost. The commitment of the present office staff to maintaining the wrenches on the counters can be explained in terms of the fact that they are positively sanctioned by both faculty and maintenance personnel; they avoid the abrasive situation that would occur if the faculty had to wait two weeks for a simple job the mechanics hate to do. The wrenches may have other uses as well.

Consider a historical example of a common situation in the relationship of social change to belief: Social change brings into existence a new class, which then elects some general belief system (for its utility) to which it gives commitment.

In 1185 a massive political change put political power in Japan into the hands of the Kamakura shogunate (1185–1338), so named because it resided in the city of Kamakura. The Kamakura shogunate established a national government based on an unstable feudal system. A steward appointed by the shogun was overseer of the land, military chieftain, and tax collector for each feudal demesne. These stewards oversaw the lands of absentee landlords who were at the imperial court at Kyoto and they eventually became the de facto rulers of the land.

During the Kamakura period, a military class that developed during the twelfth century was the dominant class. The relationship between the Samurai, as they were called, and their employers was not contractual but was presumably one of absolute loyalty without consideration for any kind of remuneration. The warrior "code" consisted simply of a stated obligation of one person to another, an obligation that superseded even ties to a family. During this period the shoguns instituted a bureaucratized system of law courts. The law was based on the house rules of the military class, which were, in turn, translations of Confucian ethics imported from China in the sixth century, and which emphasized the obligation of the vassal to his lord.

The beliefs of the new Samurai class consisted of Confucian loyalty to family, translated into soldier loyalty to lord. This code justified absolute obedience. It stressed athletic prowess, bravery, and "honor" as opposed to aesthetic achievement or delicacy of sentiment. "To resolve hastily to die is easy; to leave a stratagem for a myriad generations is hard,"[3] expresses both the Samurai preoccupation with glory and their disregard for self-preservation. This belief system rewarded chivalrous behavior and encouraged a consistent, nonreligious, nonmanipulative, antiintellectual asceticism. The severity of the military courts and the hardships of life spent almost exclusively in the field encouraged an athletic life devoid of the complex ritual and ceremony of the Heian era or of the Kyoto aristocracy. At the same time that the Samurai belief system developed, an older system that emphasized aesthetic achievement, sentimentality, and behavioral refinement persisted in the imperial court. The literature of the aristocracy consisted of sentimental romances and impressionist poetry, while that of the (apparently) largely illiterate Samurai consisted of chivalric tales and blood-and-guts war stories carried on in the epic verbal tradition.[4]

The end of the (previous) Heian period signaled the development of several new religions in Japan. Previously, Japanese religion had been magical and syncretistic; its social base had not been located predominantly in any one social class or interest group. It was a collection of eclectic religions, none of which aspired to catholic status. Native Shinto had blended with Confucianism and Buddhism as they were introduced into Japan. At base was the magical, manipulative orientation of an agrarian religion.

Along with the considerable revision of social structure that announced the Kamakura period, new religions were introduced and old faiths reinterpreted. Among them was Zen Buddhism, imported earlier from China. Our concern, however, is not with Chinese Zen, but with the Samurai adaptation under these emerging social conditions.

Samurai Zen was ascetic in the sense that it encouraged extreme self-discipline, stressed illumination or insight rather than rational intellectual practice, and involved learning no great body of doctrine. It stressed self-control in the face of the uncertain or the

[3]Cited in McCullogh (1959).

[4]McCullogh (1959) is an excellent example of the genre.

unpleasant. In many ways, Samurai Zen was preparation *in advance* for the exigencies of military life.

Japanese Zen had two quite different foci: as a belief system roughly congruent with the necessities of warrior life and the warrior code, and as an intellectual and aesthetic discipline. The Samurai picked up only that part of Zen congruent with the realities of the life situations faced by their class. A new social group called into existence by changes in social structure modifies an available belief system to fit its own needs by choosing to ignore such parts of the prophecy as have no utility.[5]

In this case, unlike the hypothetical example of the wrenches, the history may be reconstructed. A new class produced out of whole cloth by a change in social structure experiences a life situation the problems of which render a syncretistic agrarian religion irrelevant. A relative newcomer is selected and reinterpreted because it is rewarding in two senses: it prepares Samurai for the life they must face (or cease being Samurai), and it accords very closely with the system of law under which the Samurai live. The explanation for commitment given to a modified version of Chinese Zen is utility in a given context.

"End of the World" beliefs are another general case in which commitment, which is sometimes very high, is also given on the basis of utility, but the situation of the groups electing these beliefs differs from what we have described above. When life is punishing and precious little can be done about it, the pain may be assuaged through beliefs of many kinds, by redefining values, displacing goals, revising aspirations, denying reality, reinterpreting happiness, and so on. One kind of such belief is an eschatology that provides solace and justification through specific answers to the question, where will it all end?

Radical social change involving thwarted goals and the destruction of a group's favorable view of its place in the cosmos, and over which the group is in no realistic position to exercise control, is often accompanied by millenarian belief. Typically these beliefs

[5]Historical data are from Sansom (1931), Anesaki (1930), Holton (1938), and McFarland (1967).

spell out a denouement in which current evils are cataclysmically destroyed (often along with everything else), followed by a static condition in which traditional values are reaffirmed. The believer's life condition is converted from hopeless misery and confusion to certainty and the necessity to hold on only until the (imminent) cataclysm.

Three such social change situations all involve some disruption of an established existence and throw whole categories of persons into new and undefined (or only partially defined) circumstances. These three situations, which are among the most common, are: (1) Changes in social organization may rule out the possibility of continuing traditional ways of life. Demographic change, conquest, urbanization, and technological change are frequently responsible. (2) People may be caught between two apparently contradictory ways of life. The marginal man participates in two incompatible cultures but is at home in neither. (3) Rising expectations produced by economic or legal changes may not be met by rapidly rising rewards. This situation usually occurs when the possibilities open to a group suddenly expand, but expectations run ahead of realities or the pace of change begins to slow down.

Cohn, in *Pursuit of the Millennium*, comments on the contributions of problems in medieval social organization to the rise of millenarian belief:

> A bird's eye view suggests that the social situations in which outbreaks of revolutionary millenarianism occurred were, in fact, remarkably uniform; and this impression is confirmed when one comes to examine particular outbreaks in detail. The areas in which the age-old prophecies about the Last Days took on a new revolutionary meaning and a new explosive force were the areas which were becoming seriously over-populated and were involved in a process of rapid economic and social change. Such conditions were to be found now in one area, now in another, for in these respects the development of medieval Europe was anything but uniform. Wherever they occurred life came to differ vastly from the settled agricultural life which was the norm throughout the thousand year span of the Middle Ages. (1961:53–54)

Later, referring to the social base for millenarian movements, Cohn continues:

> Journeymen and unskilled workers, peasants without land or with too limited land to support them, beggars and vagabonds, the unemployed and those threatened with unemployment, the many who for one reason or another could find no assured and recognized place—such people, living in a state of chronic frustration and anxiety, formed the most impulsive and unstable elements in medieval society. Any disturbing, frightening or exciting event—any kind of revolt or revolution, a summons to a crusade, an interregnum, a plague or a famine, anything in fact which disrupted the normal routine of social life—acted upon these people with peculiar sharpness and called forth reactions of peculiar violence. And one way in which they attempted to deal with their common plight was to form a salvationist group under a messianic leader. (1961:59–60)

Several of the best known millenarian movements have occurred in situations in which the traditional life of a people has been interrupted or destroyed in such a manner that reintegration or the adoption of new ways is difficult or impossible. In this situation people seem prone to adopt millenarian belief.

The "Ghost Dance" offers a well documented case of the phenomenon. The Ghost Dance movement was a millenarian social movement that spread through the Plains Indian culture when that culture was well on its way toward destruction. The Plains Indian cultural life was based on an economy of hunting and intertribal warfare. The traditional rituals of the Pawnee, for instance, were largely concerned with either warfare or hunting. Lesser (1933) maintains that the truly destructive influence was not really domination by the white man but the disappearance of the buffalo and the partially effective ban on tribal warfare. In this situation the ritual props of the Pawnee life ceased to have relevance for day-to-day experience. Of what good are rituals concerned with hunting when there is nothing to hunt? The disappearance of the buffalo, of course, brought absolute want as well.

Into this situation came a prophetically announced religious movement that was resonant with older Indian religious movements. It promised that if the Indians would perform the Ghost Dance and would resurrect their old tribal games and rituals the buffalo would return, the white man would be destroyed, and Indians would be left alone in a great brotherhood. Indian ways had not disappeared but were being carried on by ancestors in a beyond. Indians should cease to imitate whites; they should recreate old ways on the basis of supernatural visions, and prepare for the new old days. The Ghost Dance was a doctrine of hope and, incidentally, of cultural revival. One of its consequences was revival of Indian culture on the basis of a millenarian promise. Restructuring occurred on the basis of a promise, of course, rather than on the basis of an actual return to buffalo hunting and institutionalized tribal warring.

The Cargo Cults of Melanesia are millenarian movements among a people whose own culture has not withstood the impact of European intrusion. For about a century millenarian movements have had both religious and political import in Melanesia. The Cargo Cults are prophetically based movements that seek by magic to force the appearance of the goods which whites bring in ships. Since the whites obviously do not produce these goods themselves, "cargo" refers to goods that miraculously appear out of the sea in ships and out of the sky in airplanes. The intrusion of Europeans, especially during World War II, was destructive to the native economy and hence to established ways of life. It brought different kinds of work and a variety of "goods" beyond the imagination of the islanders and, hence, it also brought expectations beyond fulfillment. With the departure at the end of the occupation of the easy work and the easy goods there was a revival of Cargo Cult belief. Docks were built to attract ships; a complete airstrip was hacked out of the jungle and a mock airplane was constructed. Like the Ghost Dance, the Cargo Cults involve cultural revitalizations and ethnic hostility (Burridge, 1960).[6]

[6]Revitalization movements are not restricted to tribal settings. The great nationalist revivals of the nineteenth and twentieth centuries are essentially similar phenomena, as are the Third World movements of today.

As industrial systems expand, they create upward mobility for members of a society. Rather than having to fight his way up, one is unable to fight hard enough to stay down. In post-World War II Japan, rapid industrial expansion has been accompanied by the rise of a number of new religions and a revival of interest in religion of such magnitude that one author has entitled a book on the subject *The Rush Hour of the Gods* (McFarland, 1967). The new movements are varieties on the Buddhist theme and seem to be characterized by a high degree of attention to worldly concerns. The best known, Sokka-Gakai, is highly politically oriented and promises to become a major, conservative influence in Japanese politics. Critics of the new movements view them as entirely worldly in orientation and obsessed with material ends. They seem to place a strong emphasis on the practical effects of religious practice. As far as one can say at this time, the membership in these movements seems to be overwhelmingly recruited from the new middle class, which is undergoing a strong Westernization, and is in turn, moving away from traditional Japanese culture and toward the new postwar culture (Thomsen, 1963).

In all these cases, commitment may be interpreted as resulting from the fact that the belief system adopted is more rewarding in some way than the ones rejected or not selected. This is not to say that millenarianism was the only option either in the Middle Ages or among the Plains Indians in the late 1880s. Nor does it mean that what is rewarding is always that which has an optimistic projected outcome.

The selection process is often described in terms of rather complex models of resonance or elective affinities.[7] These terms mean that groups under strain elect beliefs that have utility—that are rewarding, for example. This is the gist of Weber's statement that the rich are seldom satisfied to be rich; they must believe that their good fortune is justified.

The relation between collective utilities and those for specific individuals can be simple and direct, in which case a member may be committed both by individual need and group membership. But

[7]See Stark (1958:256-263) and Gerth and Mills (1958:267-301).

the relation can be enormously complex, and a member may have to decide between personal utility and conformity to group norms. It is not unusual for an individual to believe strongly "because" the belief somehow benefits a group to which he owes allegiance.

GROUP PROCESSES PRODUCING COMMITMENT—THE CAREER OF MEMBERSHIP. The process of producing commitment involves the same basic problems for all groups but requires contrasting techniques under different social circumstances. There are probably as many specific organizational devices for producing commitment as there are groups. Strategies appropriate to a Presbyterian Sunday School could be counterproductive for an underground political movement.

The commitment of an individual member of a group may be seen as a continuous progression from his recruitment to his active participation in group effort, including recruiting and socializing new members. The process begins with a personal need that is met by the belief system and its organizational vehicle, proceeds through incorporation of the individual into the group, and continues with his acquisition of an ever greater personal stake in the belief as part of his self-conception and in the organization as the locus of his activities.

Although it is convenient to speak of the organization as an active agency, it actually consists of a set of individuals collectively making decisions. Member commitment is partly a stake in decision-making. The point of maximum commitment to the organization comes when the member has maximum power: collective actions are *his.* One's career in an organization involves progressive commitment as his stake in the organization increases and as his conception of self is informed by the belief system.

1. *Recruitment.* Socially ascriptive recruitment (such as ethnicity, birth, or marriage) sets different conditions for the initial stages of progressive commitment from those present in groups that recruit by attracting potential members directly. For one thing, the personal

need that motivates initial affiliation is given by the ascriptive characteristic: small children go to church because their parents send them, members of disadvantaged ethnic minorities join organizations of their peers in part because no one else invites them, and so on. The socializing agency does not have an intrinsic and pressing motive to work with, but it does have a captive audience.

When recruitment is voluntary, however, the belief system and its social vehicle must attract members in competition with other possible memberships or with no membership at all and must therefore capitalize on some need of the prospective member.

The most general personal need available for the purpose of recruitment appears to be related to social isolation—lack of or dissatisfaction with interpersonal relationships. This can occur either because the person has deliberately broken previous ties (the postadolescent and the divorcee, for example) or because of enforced loneliness (the single man employed in an unfamiliar city). Successful recruitment in this case depends more on the group's ability to provide rewarding interpersonal relationships than on the substance of the belief system. Of the many passersby who stop to listen to a street-corner evangelist out of "curiosity," the loneliest, not the most curious, are apt to be recruited. However, as we will remark again and again, not just *any* belief system will do. The substance of the belief system is important but so are other things. Belief is clearly not a purely cerebral process, nor is it purely expedient.

The first hurdle in becoming a member is the discontinuity in self-concept involved in the transition from nonmember to member. This problem is simplified, of course, in groups that recruit through ascription, but even in these, stages of membership usually require adjustment of self-concept. Self-concept, being a largely social product, is highly amenable to social manipulation, particularly if the self is willing. Rituals call attention to, and legitimate, the transition conveying the message that there has indeed been a change but at no loss of personal integrity.

The basic ritual process is that of convincing the recruit that his social identity is sufficiently altered that behavioral consistency may proceed along new lines. This is done by signaling the moment of change, and by having representatives of appropriate social roles behave as if the change had occurred: the recruit sees his new self in the treatment others accord him. How does a young woman reconcile her virginal self-concept with her sexual companion self-concept? A minister or priest stands her up in front of her mother and father (who were responsible for the virginal self-concept) and tells her that from this moment she is a different person. If *they* accept it, so must she. Her friends, neighbors, relatives, and even people she can only vaguely identify, immediately begin to address her by a new name and title.

If the change of identity is drastic enough, the *rite de passage* may legitimate the present by dramatizing the fact that the past is hereby discarded and done with, and therefore not a basis for behavioral consistency. Ritual rebirth with a new social personality (and often a new name) may be enacted, or there may be ritual cleansing to wipe away the past, allowing the new member to proceed on a new set of premises.

Most nonascriptive recruitment involves "anticipatory socialization," that is, the recruits prepare themselves in advance by learning as much as possible about the belief system and "trying on" the beliefs in fantasy.[8]

This account of recruitment is greatly at odds with the traditional image of the dramatic conversion experience. We take conversion experiences to be instances of anticipatory socialization in which cognitive incongruity has inhibited identification with the group or belief system in question. The individual may have been in the process of becoming a believer for months or years without being altogether aware of it. The actual conversion, we suspect, is a *rite de passage* differing from other such rituals only in the fact that the participant may be largely unconscious of its ritual, conventional character.[9] It need not even be public, so long as the individual can convince himself of the legitimacy of his change of status.

[8]Most associations have some formalized means such as a course of study to provide the detailed or sensitive parts of the ideology which are not likely to be correctly learned by informal processes.

[9]Indeed, conversion experiences are often so highly conventionalized that it requires real effort not to view them as rituals learned for the occasion.

It must be emphasized that all that is ordinarily required is some way of facilitating the recruit's own desire to affiliate himself with the group. In fact, some organizations set up barriers in the way of affiliation so that recruits will not become members until their motivation is at a peak. Having expended the cost of entrance fees, the time of filling out forms and applications, the pain of initiation rites, and the energy of pleading for membership, the new member has already substantially committed himself to the organization.

The rituals surrounding recruitment and initiation are often powerful enough to be useful even in organizations where recruitment is involuntary, such as prisons or conscripted armies. Here, the recruit's previous social contacts are deliberately cut and all his daily interactions are within the institution. His previous status is systematically removed and replaced with an institutional status by the use of uniforms, titles and terms of address, and a new language. The recruit commits himself, willingly or not, by carrying out ritual behaviors (drilling, cleaning latrines, caring for his bed and uniform, answering roll call, and so on) that publicly affirm his new identity.[10]

If what we have inferred from the literature on cognitive incongruity is correct, then research on conversion ought to demonstrate that the greater the gap between what one is converted *from* and what one is converted *to*, the more painful the conversion experience should be, and the *more* likely it should be to stick. To be converted from one variety of Protestant fundamentalism to another should be neither a difficult nor a very secure conversion. Indeed, perhaps the explanation of the fact that promises made in the heat of a religious revival seem to have little effect on next Sunday's church attendance lies exactly here. To be converted from science to occultism, however, or from political pluralism to Maoism should be both painful and, if it is really carried through, lasting. To have gone through the "old" Marine Corps boot camp, *even as a draftee*, should have produced a strikingly greater percentage of lasting conversions (re-ups) than the softened "new army" is producing.

2. *Socialization.* Of the various general techniques of socializa-

[10]See Dornbusch (1955) for a detailed description of this process.

tion, the one in which we are specifically interested is calculated to produce strong commitment and independence from immediate group sanctions. It operates through initial social support, then reward and punishment based on motives learned during the period of support, and finally a set of "voluntary" actions which commit the trainee more and more deeply while he is receiving less and less social support. Ordinarily this style of socialization is practiced on a directly personal basis (such as mother-son, doctor-patient) that makes it especially powerful, but the sequence of behaviors can be applied on a fairly large scale.

At the outset, social support is provided in the form of uncritical and unconditional acceptance. This meets the social needs that motivate most recruits and serves as a basis on which to make later demands. Social approval or disapproval cannot be used to affect behavior until the new member has come to value group membership for its own sake. Socialization requires two different steps in learning. First the desire for the social reward is instilled, and next the presence or absence of the social reward is used to motivate further learning. Usually conformity is made a condition of group membership only under extreme circumstances. Expulsion from the group is the ultimate sanction and therefore to be used with care.[11]

Learning the belief system is governed by reward and punishment based on affection (approval) or its withdrawal (disapproval). This converts an interpersonal motive into commitment to a possible impersonal belief. This is fairly automatic where status and power in the association are accorded directly on the basis of commitment.

Rituals of membership provide consensual support and maintain the acquired social identity. The importance of their public character is the fact that the group present accepts and supports the identity in order to convince the member of its truth. Affirming a belief publicly commits one publicly, and implies that incongruent behavior will not go unobserved.

If the member belongs to more than one association, however, he is subject to potentially contradictory conditions for learning. The most powerful social condition for internalization is one in which

[11]It is used, typically, only during the early stages of an association's history.

the person belongs to several different associations, all of which sanction the same beliefs. This not only obviates cross-pressures, but obscures the specific social bases for belief and enhances the consensual basis for validation as well. Failing congruence in the beliefs fostered by different memberships, a standard organizational practice is to ban membership in associations carrying contradictory beliefs. This can be a straightforward prohibition or it can result from requiring the member to acquire characteristics or to execute acts that cause other people to refuse to associate with him.[12]

The most powerful actions for producing commitment give the believer a behavior to make his future belief consistent with and serve to cut him off from membership in other associations at the same time. Hours of practice on the trombone, for example, paradoxically produce a commitment to music through simultaneous investment of time and effort plus social isolation. A far more striking example can be found in the case of Jehovah's Witnesses. The new Witness, called a Pioneer, is required to invest a great deal of time in distributing evangelical literature and trying to convince others to give up their beliefs and accept those of the Witnesses. The sheer investment of time makes any other memberships a virtual impossibility and throws the Pioneer back on the company of other Witnesses. The continued recitation of Witness arguments makes the Pioneer polished in their use. The focus on continual evangelistic effort validates the arguments ("Why can't they see how right we are?") and the offensiveness of the arguments to most of the population reinforces social isolation (at least from dominant social groups).[13]

The process of progressive commitment may also be furthered in a piecemeal fashion by making little commitments that later lead to larger ones that are justified by already having made the little ones.

[12]Substantial empirical evidence indicates that the less political consistency in a voter's immediate personal relations, the less predictable his role and the later in the campaign he makes up his mind (Lazersfeld et al., 1948). As we have previously remarked, Simmel (1955) regarded overlapping group memberships as maximizing social control, and group memberships that crosscut each other as maximizing individuation. See also Borhek (1965).

[13]See Stroup (1945) for a discussion of the Jehovah's Witnesses.

He who raises his hand today may take communion next week, testify the week after, publicly confess his sins the next week, contribute half his wealth the next, and so on. Each act is later seen by the believer as incompatible with disbelief: He is committed to an adaptation of his own previous behavior. The more distasteful that behavior on other grounds, the more convincing it is that to deny it now would be the waste of a great investment. As a matter of fact this is exactly the process by which many people acquire Ph.D.s and other professional degrees.

Each step increasingly separates his belief from its directly social source, and binds it instead to his own behavior. In the fully socialized believer, the social source has been forgotten altogether and belief is simply a matter of personal integrity. The function of public rituals for him is not to provide a motive for believing, but simply to continue the process of consensual validation. Even when you are certain that your beliefs are your own, it is comforting to know that others are also aware of the truth.[14]

3. *Maintenance of the Belief.* The fully socialized member's belief is sustained through consensual validation and through the use of the abstract criteria of validation (as authoritatively interpreted) more or less on his own. The most powerful consensual validation to which he is subject comes from socializing new members. Also, his commitment deepens through the years by virtue of the time and effort he has committed to the belief and by virtue of the other commitments he has *not* made during the period.

Crises arise, to be met with the same basic techniques, based on the same personal commitments. When belief is seriously threatened, the member may find himself so committed that he or she is willing to consider almost any alternative rather than disbelief: (1) Years of belief tend to automatically narrow the person's alternatives. Having devoted 10 years to a dull marriage and four children, for example, one is unable to return to the oat-sowing stage. The alternatives are to justify one's family by continued belief or to have one's life turn to ashes. (2) The memberships associated with belief

[14]Hence the incongruous fact that the converted proclaim their voluntary turn to God in such highly stereotyped language.

are apt to produce social interests. One may join a church in a religious frenzy, and meet business partners and clients who lead to prosperity. In later years the frenzy may subside, but leaving the church would endanger the prosperity. (3) Intense personal relationships are often formed on the basis of belief. When the belief is shaken, the fact that your husband and sons would leave you for apostasy tends to shore up the belief. (4) Personal integrity is at stake. The possibility that one has been a gullible idiot and consequently a public fool for 20 years is unpalatable.[15]

Obviously there is a circular interplay between belief and social organization. Interest in a belief motivates a friendship, which commits one to the belief, which provides a stronger basis for the friendship, thereby making it more difficult to back out of the belief, and so on. It is not so much reciprocal causation as it is a repetitive process through time. One's social position during one interval sets the conditions for his belief during the second, which sets the conditions for his social position during the third, and so on. Commitment phenomena also tend to be cumulative, as one basis for commitment tends to produce others in the next time interval. Developing a reputation as a flying saucer nut, for example, results in fewer invitations from conventional boys, which makes association with unconventional boys more attractive, which actually repels conventional boys.

Paradoxically, a serious threat to belief, such as a dramatic failure, tends to result in a *higher* level of commitment within an organization.[16] Consider a political party that has just lost an election. Marginal members are immediately driven out by the failure. The smaller group of the faithful who remain are strongly committed socially or in terms of belief or both, and can therefore provide intense social support for one another. The fact of having supported the losing cause in itself tends to make believers feel rejected by other members of the society, and their resulting behavior tends to produce some actual rejection. The actions they

[15]See Crossman (1949) for a series of autobiographical studies of commitment and its dissolution.

[16]See Festinger (1956) for a study and bibliography on this topic.

have taken to incur this rejection give them a vested interest in having been "right." Their response is often to proselytize, which functions to sustain belief no matter what its outcome. First, attempting to persuade strengthens belief in itself. Second, if the persuasion is unsuccessful, the result is further rejection by the outside world, increasing dependence on the movement. Third, a successful persuasion (even if unusual) provides strong consensual validation: "If I convinced him, I *must* be right."

4. *Organizational Power and Status.* Seniority is a stratifying principle with almost universal recognition. Years of devotion are by no means the only cause of power, honor, and position within an organization, but other things being equal, commitment to the organization and to the belief system generally implies a reward in respect at least, if not in decision-making power as well. Where other things are not equal—where ability, resources, connections, training, and so forth assume greater importance than seniority—it is usually because other skills are in greater demand and scarcer supply than loyalty. In any case, commitment to the organization and its beliefs is so valuable for the purposes of collective action that it is probably never disregarded entirely in the selection of leadership.

In any given organizational career the point of maximum power usually comes quite late, and in any leadership group senior members tend to be overrepresented in relation to their numbers in the total membership. This does not imply that all or even most devoted long-time members are rewarded with office, but it does mean that new members can look forward to an increasing probability of such reward with increasing seniority, and that leaderships tend toward some degree of domination by seniority.

Honor, and especially power, are doubly committing. They are rewarding and constitute a stake in the organization. They identify self-concept with organizational office by making the man responsible for organizational decisions, and by further obscuring the social source of his belief. Most important, they are a social act the member must include in his struggle for personal integrity: being granted a position by other members, one takes on the burden of living up to it.

This is the final step in progressive commitment. In social life generally, the way to invite commitment from another is to pledge it yourself. In directly interpersonal terms, commitment is power, and the way for A to request power over B is to announce B's power over A: This is one reason for saying "I love you." Organizationally, granting a position of power is an invitation to maximum commitment.

GROUP PROCESSES PRODUCING COMMITMENT—LIMITATION OF ALTERNATIVES. Every association that carries a belief evolves a set of processes for ensuring the maximum degree of member commitment. Apart from the career of progressive commitment, the most general such social process is that of structuring the member's alternatives so that he has little choice in the matter of belief.

Much of human social behavior may be explained by the simple fact that social environments severely limit the range of choice available to an individual or to a population. Outlaw groups are of course the extreme example. They appear to recruit from those who have no other alternatives. Once recruited, for whatever reason, the member is stigmatized and finds it difficult to leave. The principle applies in more dilute form however and appears to be one of the major social bases of commitment. It may be that a given commitment is not a terribly attractive proposition, but the individual has no realistic chance of core membership in the Chamber of Commerce, the Friends of Music, or the Republican Central Committee. Every urban resident is supposed to have full access to all the social roles of his community but, in fact, the alternatives actually available to any adult are severely restricted.[17] Gilbert and Sullivan's satiric hymn praises this type of commitment: "yet in spite of all temptations/ to belong to other nations/ he remains an Englishman."

Two very general principles of limitation—cutting off information that might invalidate the belief, and building dependence on the belief, the association, or both—are called *encapsulation* and

[17]See Abramson et al. (1958) and Thompson (1967) on this point.

entanglement. It should be understood that they are separated for analytical purposes and in reality will never be found entirely independent of each other.

1. *Encapsulation.* This is a process in which possible invalidation is reduced in probability by building walls between the believer and the outside world, thereby reducing the input of uncontrolled information. The more extreme the control the association seeks over the individual member, the more energy will be invested in maintaining control over the information the individual receives. At one pole is the withdrawing religious order or sect, or the prison, which seeks almost absolute separation between its members and the outside world. At the other pole is the highly secularized organization that expects and can tolerate a fairly low degree of commitment to the belief system and a fairly high turnover of members (Selznick, 1960).

Many religious orders and sects practice some form of *isolation,* removing themselves physically from contact with unbelievers. This process is frequently consciously perceived as a group goal with full knowledge of the social functions of isolation. The Hutterian Brethren in Canada live on communally owned farms in the midst of the Canadian prairies. The new communards of the 1960s and 1970s have settled primarily, although not exclusively, in the less densely populated areas of the United States. Religious orders have frequently been able to produce isolation through a combination of high walls and/or norms that make continued membership conditional upon avoiding outside contacts. Organizations seeking quick and drastic changes in the way their members see themselves and the world isolate them physically and socially. Military training organizations typically restrict the new recruit to quarters and restrict his mail for a period of time and then, in the case of organizations training a military elite, carefully supervise his social contacts thereafter.[18] The process of brainwashing involves isolation from the outside world and careful manipulation of the information that comes through—in the Korean War, for instance,

[18]See Dornbusch (1955), and also Kanter (1968).

"Dear John's" and duns from collection companies were always delivered, whereas supportive letters were withheld (Lifton, 1961). In a thoroughly banal way, sororities in American colleges can also be described as functioning, by intent, to produce isolation from contaminating influences.

Insulation is a process that puts barriers between members and contaminating persons and ideas, but that is not dependent on physical separation of members and outsiders. Insulation may consist of specific beliefs which function to discredit information coming from the outside. A good example of this is the "peculiar people" belief so common in sects. This belief says that "we" are "different" and that this "difference" is a product of "our" having rejected a corrupt world. "Come ye out and be ye separate" is a command to reject and therefore discredit the "world." A similar function was performed by the norm in American college sororities that prohibited members, at the penalty of public censure, from associating with males who were not members of fraternities. Membership was not conditional upon endogamous "dating," but contacts with contaminating influences from a lower caste were punished by some form of disapproval by other members.

Stacking is a process in which members are involved in layers of association, each one of which reinforces the belief system, and participation in which precludes participation in associations that transmit other beliefs. Church groups typically involve their members in a number of time-consuming voluntary associations that reinforce commitment by increasing exposure to dogma and build personal identity through heavy interaction with other members. In nation-states that demand belief as well as conformity, one is typically involved from nursery school through retirement in organizations that transmit politically approved content. Thus, in each of the associations in which an individual participates, a uniform set of beliefs is socialized. When contrasted with the situation generally characterized as urban in which the multiple memberships of given individuals are conflicting and crosscutting, the power of stacking in producing conformity becomes apparent (Simmel, 1950).

2. *Entanglement.* In this process, commitment to an association

and a belief system is increased by making the member's life and self indistinguishable from the association or belief. We have previously commented on some entangling procedures in associations, such as rewarding commitment with power or prestige. There are many such devices that seek either to *label* the member or to *build dependence.* By far the most common labeling device is the one in which the believer is asked to make a public statement that he will then have to defend. The public confession was used by the early phase of Moral Rearmament. People were invited to "house parties" and in the warmth and congeniality of the atmosphere were encouraged to confess various small embarrassing sins before other guests, thereby demonstrating a "need" for Moral Rearmament (Eister, 1950). Behavior of this kind is customary in sectarian churches in which the testimonial is an accepted form—to demonstrate my commitment I publicly testify to my salvation, which strengthens other's views of my commitment and hence provides standards for me to live up to. The Hare Krishna movement of the early 1970s requires an unusually permanent form of public statement—shaving one's hair back to a topknot. Tatooing is a common form of demonstrating commitment to an association. Its history as a device for publicly stating one's loyalty to an association or a belief (Death before Dishonor) or to a fellowship (the pachuco) goes back most indefinitely.

Dependence on the association also commits the member to the belief. Hunter S. Thompson, in *Hell's Angels* (1967), provides an interesting journalistic analysis of recruitment and commitment to an outlaw motorcycle gang that has a substantial belief system of fairly high system and very high empirical relevance. Commitment to the association and hence to the belief tends to be negative in character. The picture Thompson provides is that members are thrown back on each other because no one else will have them. They become unemployable in regular working-class jobs because of court records, their social behavior challenges the most relaxed standards, and they are unable to leave the Angel fold. Commitment to the belief is generated in considerable part by the inability of members to survive outside of the association.

Another device by which associations build commitment to themselves and to beliefs is the establishment of systems of rank and status that do not reflect the stratification system institutionalized in the larger society. This common feature of quasi-secret associations provides rewards of high status to persons whose occupational or ethnic status in the larger society may be low.

SUMMARY. Nothing else is really important to the social vehicle that carries a belief system if it cannot generate commitment. A belief system with no members has interest only to antiquarians. If commitment can be made high enough, however, a belief system and its social vehicle may survive even a gross failure of validation. What then are the social bases of the commitment of members?

We have argued that the social bases of commitment may lie in the biography of the individual, in procedures the association takes to try to generate commitment among members, and in procedures the organization takes to prevent members from encountering other belief systems and associations. An obvious inference is that a corpus of committed believers is not produced out of thin air by a single device, nor is their commitment sustained by the obvious rightness of the belief, but that a series of elements operating in an additive manner are responsible for commitment. It is a fairly safe hypothesis that no matter how much it may seem to be the other way, all strong commitments are products of a number of factors and this number grows over the career of any given member.

The Validation of Belief

The social power of belief depends on what Durkheim called its *external* quality; belief systems seem, to believers, to transcend the groups that carry them, to have an independent existence of their own.[1] For belief systems to persist, that is, they must not only motivate commitment through collective utility but also through making the belief system itself seem to be valid in its own right. This chapter investigates how this appearance of intrinsic validity is preserved.

[1]On this general topic, see Durkheim (1965), Berger and Luckmann (1968:85-118), and Holzner (1968:41-59). Much of the literature on reality construction is concerned with this point.

The validation of belief is a largely social process in spite of the requirement that if the validating device were perceived as *merely* social, it would be inadequate. Perceived consensus is not in itself a sufficient condition for the social power of belief. Therefore validation is not simply a matter of organizational devices for the maintenance of member commitment (treated in Chapter 5), but also of the social arrangements whereby the abstract system of belief is accorded validity in terms of its own criteria.

One of the subtlest yet most powerful influences of social life on thought is simply that the appropriate criteria for determining validity or invalidity are socially defined. Logics and proofs are just as much social products as the beliefs they validate. Surely, an idea is valid if it objectively passes the criterion of validity itself! But the criterion of validity is chosen consensually and it is applied through a series of social conventions.[2]

Two factors introduce nonsocial elements into the process of validation. First, the belief system has a *logic* of its own, which may not lead where powerful members of the group want it to. The second factor is the *pressure of events,* happenings in the real world that may bring pressure on believers to relinquish a belief. Successful circumnavigation of the earth brings into question its flatness, for example; the death of a loved one brings into question either the goodness or the omnipotence of God; and military failure brings into question the legitimacy of a regime.

The specific topics of this chapter are, first, the characteristics of the belief system itself which make it more or less susceptible to the buffets of the real world; second, the means by which group membership supports the credibility of belief; and third, commonly encountered strategies of validation.

CHARACTERISTICS OF THE BELIEF SYSTEM WHICH AFFECT VALIDATION. For a belief system to survive the pressure of events with enough member commitment to make it powerful, it

[2]Berger and Luckmann (1968) have discussed the issue of "legitimation" at some length. See their discussion for an alternative to ours.

must receive (or seem to receive) validation beyond the level of mere consensus. For a member to believe that the simultaneous commitment of other believers provided the only valid basis of his belief would be cynicism. Of course some, and even a majority, of the believers may be cynics (consider the social context of contemporary belief in Santa Claus), but if *all* are cynics, the external power of the belief system is lost altogether. The power of a belief system, then, depends on its ability to validate itself in the face of reason for doubt.

Belief systems are not all equally well equipped to deal with the problem of validation. By virtue of its structure, a belief system may be able to fend off negative evidence in a given environment but experience difficulty as social conditions change. Belief systems may respond to a changing environment not only with adjustments in the social vehicles that carry them, but also with changes in the logic affecting validation.

Belief systems vary in the logical interrelatedness of their substantive beliefs (degree of system) *and in the extent to which those beliefs pertain directly to the empirical world* (empirical relevance). These two variable characteristics of belief systems directly affect the ease with which a given belief system can be validated, or invalidated, as it confronts the continual pressure of events.

The mind of man is sufficiently fertile that any belief system *could* operate through a strong logic and *could* be made relevant to empirical events. If a belief system is not systematic *or* empirically relevant it is because the community of believers has chosen not to make those connections. One possible reason not to make them is to make the belief system almost invulnerable to negative evidence.

Consider the possibilities that are open when a belief is challenged by events. First, the belief may be discarded, or at least the level of commitment reduced. Second, the belief may be affirmed in the very teeth of events—the "triumph of faith"—which must represent consensual validation of some sort. Third, the believers may deny that the events were relevant to the belief, or that the particular belief that was challenged was importantly related to the rest of the belief system. In other words the alternative response may be in terms of the empirical relevance or the systematic quality of the belief system itself.

Nonempirical, unsystematic belief systems are more resistant to the pressure of events than empirical, systematic beliefs. Beliefs may refer to a nonempirical plane in such a way that one's life may be guided by them, but also in such a way that no empirical event (by definition) can contradict them. Conversion experiences are an example. The converted often express the feeling of an almost physical intimacy with the deity that profoundly alters their behavior and their views of self and others. Such experiences are as real to those who experience them as day and night. Still, the experience involves a belief that does not encounter empirical reality even though it may in the long run affect it. Similarly, the belief system may be so general, have so many possible interpretations, or so few *necessary* connections between beliefs that neither empirical events nor textbook logic can contradict the system itself. An example here is mysticism. Since belief systems may vary independently along these two dimensions, commitment may be protected either way or by both simultaneously.

Negative evidence—whatever renders belief implausible—may be external to the belief system and its organizational vehicle, or it may be internal. When a prophecy fails and the world does not end, when the Second Coming does not occur, or the faithful are not carried off in flying saucers, believers are confronted with external evidence.[3] Internal evidence consists of data which derive from the belief system itself or from an organization to which it is attached. A lecturer on "Better Pay Through Interpersonal Competence," for example, may come to dread the inevitable question, "If you so smooth, how come you ain't rich?" When the prophet is arrested for pederasty or the ascetic guru is discovered to have ordered a Rolls Royce, another kind of internal evidence must be faced that may have nothing to do with the abstract belief system. It severely strains credibility nonetheless.

For highly systematic belief, any attack upon any of its principles

[3]See Festinger et al. (1956) for a participant-observer research of a case of this type and for examples drawn from historical literature.

is an attack upon the system itself; if one principle is abandoned, all the others must be, too. Therefore, *the greater the degree of system, the greater the importance of negative evidence for the whole belief system.* A syncretistic belief system can withstand attacks on any of its parts because they are only loosely connected to each other. If one of the basic propositions of a systematic belief system is brought under attack, then so is the entire system. In consequence, a systematic belief system is at the mercy of its weakest element. But to apply the notion of system to concrete cases, it is necessary to remember that it is the systematic quality of beliefs *as they are believed and used,* not as they *might be used,* that is important. Ordinarily, for example, we should think of highly organized Catholicism, with its history of scholasticism, as systematic, and of loosely organized Protestantism, with its history of internal schism, as unsystematic. But "system is as system does," and believers may treat Catholicism unsystematically and Protestantism systematically, as in the following example.

In 1970 Pope Paul VI decanonized a number of saints, including Saint Christopher. This did not threaten the entire belief system. The sainthood of Christopher is tied only by a relatively weak, a posteriori, logic to the dogma of the bodily assumption of the Virgin Mary, which is only weakly tied to the idea of the moral infallibility of the Pope. Roman Catholicism has weathered severe attacks—including those that may lead to rejection of the dogma of papal infallibility—and probably will continue to weather them, because these separate beliefs are linked together by history, tradition, and authority rather than by some unavoidable inner logic.[4] The same authority that establishes dogma may disestablish it. Furthermore, many Catholic dogmas have little empirical relevance. What kind

[4]We recognize the fact that this statement flies in the face of much (especially Catholic) scholarly opinion but would argue that the enormous effort that has been exerted to *produce* the appearance of system has been both after the fact and has had relatively little connection with religion as it appears in its concrete form among lay believers in the field, much less with the "growing edge" of Catholicism in, let us say, an isolated village in the state of Jalisco, Mexico. This is *not* to say that all dogmas are of equal importance, however. A challenge to the authority or charter of the church itself would probably undermine the whole structure.

of event could challenge the dogma of the Assumption of the Virgin Mary into Heaven or the loose set of beliefs sometimes called Maryism?

On the other hand, Ascetic Protestantism, that loose congery of churches which espouses puritan norms in one state or another of decay, shows great system in the manner in which beliefs are held. Such puritanism can probably be reduced to three basic axioms from which all specific beliefs can be deduced with no further assumptions: spontaneous emotion is evil, man is a tool of divine purpose, and no thought or act is irrelevant. How shall we handle grief? Suppress it because spontaneous emotion is evil. How shall we organize our services? Without ritual or ceremony because they are nonrational. How shall we judge habitual practices that emerge out of social interaction? On the basis of utility. What art is "good art?" Either none, because art is nonrational, or art that instructs in useful sentiments. One of these basic dogma is currently under severe attack—clearly two of the strongest implications of the hip life-style are that "if it feels good it *is* good" and that a person should "do his own thing." This rejection of the puritan avoidance of personal pleasure is manifest on a wide front, from women's and men's magazines that openly sell the guiltless pursuit of individual pleasure to mass audiences, to "encounter groups" in churches. A highly systematic belief system is like an arch. If the key is removed the whole structure falls, and one of the keys of puritanism is presently very loose.

Unsystematic belief systems permit much greater dissension among believers because the existence of disagreement is hard to demonstrate. A systematic belief system has powerful conceptual properties, but those very properties highlight the smallest disagreement and give it importance in its logical connections with other items of belief.[5] The great debate over the appearance of navels in

[5]Even if a systematic belief system is entirely nonempirical, it is vulnerable because even one shaken belief can lead to the loss of commitment to the entire structure. This point is nicely illustrated in contrasting reactions of the Pawnee and the Comanche to culture contact. The more highly integrated Pawnee culture fell apart like the one-hoss shay because of the importance of the interrelationships among the

religious paintings would never have occurred if the logical connection between the Adam and Eve story and belief in God had not been drawn so strongly at that time.

A belief system with relatively little reference to the empirical world cannot be much affected by external empirical evidence simply because the events of this world do not bear upon it. The continued evangelical belief in the mercy of God can scarcely be challenged by the continued wretchedness of life, because the two never meet. *The less the degree of empirical relevance, the less the importance of external evidence, but the greater the importance of internal evidence.*

The manner in which nonempiricism may be used to protect commitment may be illustrated by the "retreat" of religion before science in Western culture. All of the adaptations to increasing scientific knowledge as a challenging event have been evidenced. Some beliefs have been dropped; some churches have, at least for a time, increased their demands for conformity of belief (consensual validation); the necessity of logical connections between dropped beliefs and the remaining religious system has been denied, and so on. Most significantly, churches have renounced claims to the immediate empirical validity of many beliefs, removing the plane of validity beyond the ability of science to contradict it. Usually this has meant that the institution of science has produced a belief that replaced a belief from the institution of religion, and that the theory that explains or justifies the belief is now scientific rather than religious. The new "religious" belief system makes no continued claim on validity in the empirical world, just as the new "scientific" belief makes no claim on validity outside the empirical world.

Concrete belief systems are directly subject to both internal and external evidence. A young political activist may become disillusioned either when he discovers dandruff on his candidate's coat or when an election is lost, though neither logically implies the abstract invalidity of his cause. The abstract ideal form of a belief

various parts of culture. Lack of system provided flexibility in the response of Comanche culture to change; new elements could combine with or replace old ones by virtue of the weak connections among the elements. See Linton (1936:364-365).

system, however, is in some measure protected from external evidence by its very nature. A cult under fire may be able to preserve its belief system only by retreating to abstraction: "Our leaders do seem to have been swindlers, but their basic ideas were valid anyway." Thus negative external evidence may motivate system-building at the level of the abstract ideal, where internal evidence is far more important.

The suprasocial force of a belief system derives most significantly from its abstract ideal form. Paradoxically, the current social influence of a belief system derives from its concrete form. A cult may overcome negative external evidence by emphasizing social benefits of membership, such as the abilities and status position of its believers—witness the attractiveness and respectability of Christian Science despite the continued prosperity of medicine. Alternatively, a cult may retreat from negative external evidence by emphasizing the abstract ideal. Either way, the change of emphasis has profound implications for long-range cult development because the type of relationship between the belief system and its organization vehicle has been altered.

The separability of the abstract belief system from its concrete expression depends on the ability of persons not affiliated with the association or unspecialized structure that carried it socially to understand and use it. Almost inevitably, this implies that *the more systematic and empirically relevant a belief system is, the greater the feasibility of preserving it as an abstract ideal apart from a given concrete expression.* In other words, the more a belief system depends on a specific person or persons for interpretation, the less it can "stand alone." If its validation comes from empirical events and the ability to systematically relate propositions according to an internally consistent logic, it can be reconstructed and perpetuated by any social group with only a few hints. Science is such a belief system. The logic of experiment can be applied by anyone who knows it, regardless of his or her connection with one of the traditional science-carrying institutions. One reason we know more about the astronomy and mathematics of the ancient Mayas than we do about their religion or folk beliefs is that the latter are in much greater need of interpretation by a priest or a grandmother.

System and empiricism, then, protect a belief system from its friends. *The greater the degree of system and the greater the degree of empiricism, the less the reliance on internal evidence and the greater the reliance on external evidence.* By the same token, these qualities make a belief system particularly vulnerable to the pressure of events. In practice, the adaptation of any belief system is some sort of compromise between the need for consensual validation and the need for independence from the fellowship or association that carries it.

By cross-classifying system and empiricism, we can generate a typology of belief systems in terms of different problems of validation. A successful solution to the problem of validation would be one that facilitated the value element in the belief system but nevertheless kept commitment high enough by allowing the abstract criteria of validity to protect crucial beliefs within the conditions imposed by the actual social environment.

1. Belief systems that are both highly systematic and highly empirical are highly vulnerable to the pressure of events, yet highly independent of their concrete forms and the particular groups which carry them. The entire system is either challenged or supported by each new piece of evidence. Validation is relatively safe in the hands of any believer who takes the trouble to become an adept, so that the destruction of a particular group, or a particular failure of charisma should not be expected to harm the abstract ideal permanently. Scientific theories are, of course, the most familiar belief systems of this type.

2. Belief systems with low empirical relevance but a high degree of system are especially vulnerable to internal evidence, and are likely to be destroyed as a piece rather than whittled away. Such belief systems require strong social support and can be expected to survive or fail largely on the basis of the charisma of the prophet or on the maintenance of consensus through institutional means. Paranoia, either as a characteristic of a person or, more importantly for us, as it appears in conspiracy theories of history is an example of this type. The authority structure (sometimes concealed from neophytes and outsiders) has, by definition, the only legitimate interpretation of the system's logic, so that the attempt to point out

internal inconsistencies is doomed. By the same token, these belief systems are particularly vulnerable to organizational or institutional attack: Once the authority has been questioned, the whole logical structure collapses like a house of cards. Crossman's *The God That Failed* (1949) contains autobiographical statements by exmembers or fellow travelers of the Communist Party. The abstract belief system, which was highly systematic, was also based on an eschatological view of history that had relatively little direct empirical relevance. In each case, the believers became disaffected *not* through invalidation of the abstract belief system but through an insight into the ulterior motive of the Party, which led to the destruction of the Party's authority in the eyes of the believer.

3. A belief system with great empirical relevance but little system is carried only by an unspecialized structure—unlike the two previous types, which are always carried by associations as well—and is extremely persistent over time though constantly changing in detail, each belief being vulnerable to external evidence. Such a belief system is immune to internal evidence, either logical inconsistency (irrelevant) or social discreditation (the organizational vehicle is too diffuse to be discredited). Superstition or other types of folk science or medicine are of this type. Quantities of specific beliefs regarding important aspects of worldly life such as farming, health, love, fertility, and success have no underlying theory. Beliefs such as "toads cause warts," "bull snakes milk cows," and "full moon is the best time to plow" have few mutual implications; if destroyed, they fall one at a time through empirical disproof or lack of consensus. Since empirical disproof is hard to come by in daily life, and since an unspecialized structure is not an appropriate organization for the diffusion of a scholar's technical paper, the perpetuation of this type of belief system is almost entirely a matter of consensual validation.

4. A number of general types of belief systems are low on both system and empirical relevance. The most common are the agrarian religions that have existed throughout the world and that are syncretistic, tolerant, and carried by an organizational vehicle. This vehicle may contain sundry fellowships and fragments of associa-

tions, but nothing approaching the usual meaning of the word "church."

Belief systems of this type, such as the hip life-style of the late 1960s, are often indicators of social change and indicate a retreat from established culture and the appearance of serious contradictions in this culture.

The relevance of this typology to research in beliefs lies in its usefulness in clarifying the kinds of validation problems faced by belief systems. Validation is not merely a matter of consensus but also of the kind of logic which exists in the various substantive beliefs. Belief systems adapt (or fail to adapt) to strains that occur in their social vehicles or in their confrontations with the real world in very different ways, and the logic of their substantive beliefs effects this adaptation.

CONSENSUAL VALIDATION—SOCIAL SUPPORT FOR COMMITMENT TO BELIEF. No social explanation is required in cases where beliefs have face validity. Many beliefs are, in fact, supported directly through personal experience in the world as it is, and the regularity of such experiences can explain belief. We believe that water is wet, that rocks are hard, and that night follows day because we are continually reassured by experience.

Yet, people believe even when events or experience do *not* validate or support belief. In fact, commitment to a belief may be even stronger when it has to be asserted in the very teeth of events than when all is right with the world.[6] How is commitment sustained in spite of the pressure of events to deny belief?

The source of support for beliefs that are not continually validated through experience is preeminently social. Group membership provides a convincing force outside the individual, who may be personally beset by doubt. In effect, if it seems that water is not wet, that rocks are not hard, or that night does not follow day, one's

[6]Eric Hoffer (1951) once asserted that to be believable a dogma had to be absurd. We are arguing a variation on this theme (with qualification) here. See also Festinger et al. (1956) for examples.

immediate and natural response is to seek support in the agreement of other humans. That is, ideas that do not receive regular support in personal experience may receive *consensual validation.* In fact the "conformity" experiments and field reports indicate that consensual validation often overrides personal experience, at least so far as public statements are concerned.[7]

At an even more general level, most of our knowledge of the world and our very manner of perceiving and thinking depends on consensual validation. The philosopher Kant stated theoretically what is today an experimental commonplace: Reality is not encountered directly, but only through socially learned styles of perception and categories of thought. In practical terms, it is difficult for a contemporary human to think of any personal experience that is so direct and unmediated by symbolic expression that he does not depend on the agreement of others for certainty. And if an experience is to be communicated, it must be transformed by the very process of symbolic expression.

How do humans develop attachments to ideas? The answer is that at some point commitment to an idea stems from relationships with one or more other humans. This point may be obvious, as in the case of a wife who had to believe as her husband did in order to retain his love and who expressed her continued love for him after his death by constant faith in his beliefs. But many of the specific social relationships responsible for commitment to some idea may not be obvious at all. Ideas generated or learned in one social setting come to have an importance of their own outside that setting. The psychological reasons for an individual's continued commitment, therefore, may be independent of the social conditions in which he acquired a belief. What is first learned socially, for example, is the very meaning of an emotional attachment, so that one's relationship with his father may later serve as a model for his relationship to an idea, even if his father opposes that particular

[7]See for example Asch (1958) and Sherif (1958). In these often repeated experiments, subjects' reports of their perceptions of apparently moving lights or of the length of lines are clearly influenced or distorted by group consensus. William F. Whyte (1943) reports a fascinating example of the influence of group norms on members' perceptions of their own bowling abilities.

idea. Thus, one of the most interesting aspects of student radicalism of the late 1960s was that the militants were, as a group, characterized by strong positive relationships with their parents and came from politically liberal, morally concerned backgrounds. Apparently, the liberal "establishment's" concern with moral issues contributed to radical action against it, as students discovered that the verbalized values of America were ignored or violated in practical action.[8]

We cannot overemphasize that commitment to ideas is not a purely cerebral process. Insofar as there is unified social life, the members of a group are committed to one another, to the group as a whole, and to the culture of the group. It is the same kind of commitment in each case, and each of these commitments is relevant to the other two. To the extent that a man rejects the culture of a group, the other members of the group understand him to reject them personally and the group collectively. To deviate without disruption of social ties, one must communicate the full message, "I am loyal, and I love you all, but . . ." Otherwise deviance is tantamount to treason.

Group membership involves a potentially revocable social contract: each member accepts a measure of control in return for the predictable social order that results from the same control over other members. Deviance in belief is threatening because it implies loss of that predictable social order through the ineffectiveness of social control over the deviant. This would leave conforming members in the worst of all possible worlds: controlled, but unable to rely on the social order. The literature on brainwashing suggests that producing exactly this situation is a most important tactic of the brainwashers (Lifton, 1961).

The process of consensual validation, then, ties the content of beliefs to the social order itself. If the social order remains, then the beliefs must somehow be valid, regardless of the pressure of events. If the beliefs are agreed upon by all, then the social order is safe. Conversely a threat to one is ipso facto a threat to the other.

The extent of commitment to belief varies directly with the

[8]Kenniston (1968:297-325) has a summary of findings on who becomes an activist.

amount of consensual validation available, and inversely with the pressure of events, other things being equal. That is, commitment is the resultant of two forces acting in opposite directions: social support, which maintains belief, and problems posed by "existence," which threaten belief. The power or confidence in action that beliefs provide stems, therefore, from group membership and participation in group life.

Some validation is provided simply by the knowledge of consensus. But when belief is shaken, further evidence of consensus is required. This can be provided by social rituals of various sorts, which may have any manifest content, but which act to convey the additional messages: (1) the group and its social order remain intact, and your place in the group is secure, (2) we still agree concerning the relevant beliefs, and (3) the implicit contract is therefore unrevoked. Each member, in publicly committing himself through ritual is rewarded by the public commitment of the others. Patriotic ceremonies on the Fourth of July are classic examples of this. Such ceremonies typically involve a formal restatement of the ideal belief system in speeches, as well as rituals that give opportunities for individual reaffirmation of commitment, such as the pledge of allegiance. The real meaning of the controversy over the use of prayer in public schools and the continuing dispute over teaching the evolution of species in high school biology courses is almost certainly not religious but has to do with a problem of retaining consensus on "traditional" American values: hard work, nationalism, conformity to a small-town life-style, and so forth, all of which are currently being challenged by hedonism, internationalism, and urban life-styles, symbolized by the secularization of education.

The same process is nevertheless characteristic of complicated social structures as well, as we show later in this chapter. Chapter 8 specifically examines validation in heterogeneous urban settings.

In *The Elementary Forms of the Religious Life* (1965), Durkheim concluded that religious behavior could be rendered sociologically intelligible by assuming an identity between society itself and the object of worship. The belief that eating the totem under ordinary circumstances produces illness, but *not* eating the totem at certain festivals leaves one weak and defenseless is assumed to represent the *same thing* as a statement affirming membership in the clan and placing reliance on it.

Thus consensual validation and validation according to abstract criteria are indistinguishable in the extreme case. If a certain belief has as its sole raison d'être affirmation of group membership, then no amount of logical or empirical proof is even relevant to validation, though proofs may in fact be emphasized as part of the ritual of group life. The social response to a statement about such a belief has more to do with the status of the speaker in relation to the group than it does with the content of the statement. Is he an outsider? One of our leaders? A brother? A renegade? Since the meaning of a totemic belief is *entirely* defined by the group, the observer's only clue to the meaning of such a belief lies in the social response to statements about it.

An example may clarify this point. Fraternal organizations as an ordinary practice establish a series of passwords, handgrips, and esoteric knowledge which appear to have as their main function identifying members vis-à-vis nonmembers or establishing the rank of members inside the organization. Validity of such knowledge is not crucial because it serves ritual functions. How can a password be "wrong"? One either knows it, in which case one is identified as a brother, or one does not know it, in which case one is identified as an outsider. The ritual of handgrips and symbols, of examinations on esoteric knowledge to attain intraorganization prestige, and all the secret and ceremonial trappings so characteristic of fraternal orders are devices that increase consensual validation in a situation in which consensual validation and validation by abstract criteria are quite indistinguishable.[9] To a worldly observer, the rituals of fraternal orders may seem childish and rather irrelevant. This appearance of irrelevance exists solely because fraternal orders are not institutions of central importance in this century. The intellectual who sneers at the Masons one day may march in an academic procession the next and take the whole thing quite seriously.

Symbols of group existence are not to be trifled with because the

[9]The classic discussion of secret societies is in Simmel (1950:345-376).

appropriate response to a personal attack is a fight, not a conversation. Being members, we could generate polite debate within the sociological fraternity by taking, in this book, certain controversial positions. But we could also generate emotional attacks and personal abuse from the same colleagues by simply concluding a chapter: "all the cultural concomitants of social interaction may, therefore, be mathematically deduced from learning theory with no additional assumptions." This statement attacks the group belief in the value of the sociological fraternity. Being outside the discipline, the statement is not something one could conclude qua sociologist. If it were asserted by a psychologist or other outsider, it would be met with courteous (albeit self-interested) arguments or (more likely) simply ignored. If we said it, it would be treason, and would be dealt with as such.[10]

STRATEGIES OF VALIDATION. Validation is the result of the maintenance of consensus and the fending off of the pressure of events in every specific case. Furthermore, every concrete belief system is at once a mixture of both the empirically relevant and nonrelevant and the systematic and unsystematic, no matter how much one side of the two dichotomies dominates. There are, therefore, a set of classic strategies by which belief systems are protected against negative evidence in the real world. Our list of these is not exhaustive, but describes commonly encountered types. Indeed, strategies of validation provide a potentially fertile field for research. The word *strategy* should not be taken to imply a self-conscious manipulation of either the logic or substantive beliefs of a system. The degree of ingenuousness is an open question to which we cannot begin to suggest an answer.

[10]Indeed, we are taking exactly such a position which will produce exactly such a response by failing to make the ritually obligatory distinction between science and silly intellectual perversions such as flying saucerism as qualitatively different kinds of knowledge. They aren't, we don't, and this violates an academic dogma as well as correcting an error that has gotten a number of sociologists of knowledge in trouble. See Taylor (1958) on Mannheim. Others who have taken the same position we do are Kuhn (1970) and Polanyi (1958).

which contemporary empirical sociology has developed is that the application of the principles of natural science will produce empirically validated lawlike statements about human social behavior. This is an empirically relevant belief that must survive the buffets of the real world. It is challenged by critics who say our theories are in disarray and tend not to be empirically relevant, that no lawlike empirically validated statements have been produced, and that even individual findings are seldom reliable or unchallenged and virtually never show relationships of any impressive magnitude. The answer to critics is usually that our discipline is young and our methods not yet developed. Just wait patiently and we will show you marvels. This is an empirically nonrelevant belief that serves to protect an empirically relevant belief from the pressure of events by indefinitely forestalling a moment of truth. There is no way to invalidate an open-ended promise—it simply does not confront the real world. Indeed, we may yet show marvels. If *we* were to abandon the defense contained in the open-ended promise, commitment to the natural science model of sociology would certainly sag. Strategies of social validation for the maintenance of commitment to belief are no less necessary in science than in religion.

The largest single category of belief systems in which empirically relevant beliefs are protected by empirically nonrelevant beliefs are those in which the primary validation derives from prophecy and/or revelation. Being intrinsically extrasocial, prophecy and revelation imply the absence of any control whatever on the person who claims the revelation. Revealed truth may fly in the face of empirical events, existing institutions, and logic alike with no court of appeal. In consequence, revelation is a type of validation which receives very gingerly treatment even in the early phases of a social movement. Established institutions are loath to accept revelation because it can make their entire system of social control irrelevant at a single stroke. Establishing a claim to revealed truth at some time in the past is one thing, but according each person the right to use his own revelation as a test of validity in the present is to tempt anarchy. Despite this, a number of social movements have had some degree of prosperity even though the belief system maintains that God speaks equally to every man. Perhaps the most interesting such group are the Doukhobors, who have traditionally had severe problems of organization and social order precisely because they deny the superiority of one person's revelation to another's (Hawthorne, 1965).

Claims of access to truth that is beyond ordinary men and to information beyond disproof make the prophet of revealed truth an important element in social change. How can the burden of tradition and the limitations of institutional social control be overcome more rapidly than by the announcement of an insight which is justified by its very being? "It is written, but I say unto you . . ." Of course, claims of this kind seldom impress anyone but him to whom it is revealed unless they are supported by some other kind of social or empirical validation. Personal charisma is what usually attracts attention to prophecy. This, of course, was exactly the point of Max Weber's *Ancient Judiasm* (1952).

2. *Using empirically relevant beliefs to validate an empirically nonrelevant thesis.* This would at first seem to contradict what we have previously said about the relatively greater danger of invalidation in which empirically relevant beliefs stand. What is different in this case is that the empirically relevant beliefs will prove out if anyone bothers to check. The empirically nonrelevant thesis must then be true as well. Few people are able to determine whether an inference from data is true or false and, under the conditions in which beliefs are presented to audiences, even those who are able to do so are unlikely to take the time. This is one of the commonplaces of the collective behavior literature. A general example should suffice. The data on secularization and the failure of social control in cities are very frequently mixed and used as the basis of inferences which are not empirically relevant. Thus it seems to be the case that the old authorities (family, church, and state) do not motivate the awe they did in the late Middle Ages. Furthermore, extensions of the power of these core institutions in sexual "morality," piety, and patriotism are not accorded the attention they were during the reign of Victoria. Furthermore, crime rates are increasing at a higher rate than population. These empirically relevant state-

ments are used to validate a considerable number of explanations which may seem plausible in one social or meaningful context or another. Thus Robert Welch of the John Birch Society states these phenomena clearly and in the context of a good deal of supportive evidence. He then attributes these phenomena to a conspiracy that goes back more than a full century and exists today. In the middle-age, middle-education, motel ballroom context in which Welch speaks, the inference seems valid and the data convincing.[12] Roughly the same data were used by former Vice President Spiro T. Agnew to validate the apparently conspiratorial existence of a group of "permissivists." A doctrinaire Marxist explanation in terms of increasing "alienation" seems to us to have as little empirical relevance as the other two. Evangelists of the last 30 years have been fond of explaining these data in terms of "moral failure" or sin.

In *Doomsday Cult* (1966), Lofland portrays this strategy most clearly. How can cult members continue to believe that the world is being destroyed and that doom is at hand? Read your daily newspaper! Every day there are crises and disasters. Floods in Pennsylvania, earthquakes in Nicaragua, mud slides in California, and riots in Paris clearly portend destruction.

That a given body of data may be interpreted in a number of ways is no secret. The point that needs making is *not* that questionable inference takes place but that the data, because of their empirical relevance, can be used to validate almost any inference, no matter how unearthly, in a sufficiently receptive context of meaning. Thus in a context of relatively limited education and relatively high wealth it is not at all surprising that the apparent deterioration of the power of the old authorities combined with the facts of crime and the increasing "intrusion" of government into the economy lend credence to a conspiratorial view of history, regardless of whether the conspirators are employees of the Department of State, college professors, or the "Elders of Zion."

3. *The manipulation of issues or enemies to strengthen a case.* Classic mechanisms of this type, by which the credibility of

[12]Observed through participation at meetings of the JBS.

beliefs may be increased, include the lumping, dissecting, and polarization.

Group enemies (or issues) may be lumped together, and the enemy used as a motive for an attack on the issue, or the issue used as a basis for identifying the enemy. The attack may be strengthened by combining despised groups or threatening issues. To attack flouridation one may show that communists are in favor of it; to attack dentists one may show that they favor vivisection of dogs; to legitimate one's attack on an agency of the federal government one may refer to the Communist-Jewish conspiracy. In belief systems in which the major substance is hate or fear, lumping is the rule.[13]

Dissecting issues is the other side of the strategic coin from lumping and is primarily a defensive response. Still, it is an attempt to gain agreement by using the socially defined process of validation, mixing social and belief criteria to taste. For example: "I agree with many of the items of my opponent's program (showing social solidarity based on consensus), but on this one point he is wrong (hence to be treated as a deviant by speaker and audience, who agree on so many things)." The social significance of agreement or disagreement is often implicit, and often powerful for not being obvious to the audience. One protects himself by denying the identity of issue and group implied by the opponent, and then conceives for the listener a new world in which the opponent is isolated by his own intractable belief, but in which speaker and audience are united by a broad basic stratum of agreement.

An example of lumping and dissecting in action may be found in the contemporary controversy over the issues of war, social inequality whether racial or sexual, and poverty. In the radical press, these issues are combined. The logical conclusion of lumping in this case is an attack on the entire economic and political system. Such an attack gains enormous power by mobilizing a number of separate discontents under one flag and presenting a single enemy. The governmental response to this has been to dissect the issues and

[13]See Lowenthal and Guterman (1949) and Toch (1965) for extended discussions of this strategy. Toch includes a detailed social psychological analysis of conspiracy theories.

present them as a number of separate unrelated problems. War is treated as a problem of international political negotiation, poverty as a local problem, urban social disorganization as a problem of (in one incredible analysis) the structure of black families, the "welfare mess" as an administrative problem. Indeed, one interpretation of the way in which public opinion is brought to bear on governmental process is that governments act on social problems only when disaffection rises to such a degree that lumping threatens to bring down the whole house.

Another important direct connection between social organization and validation is the process of polarization. This is a means of gaining influence over others by dominating the orientation element of their belief system, that is, by controlling the categories into which they must sort empirical data. Polarization refers to clusters of ideas whose opposing positions become increasingly more extreme and contrasting, with no middle ground or compromise position possible, as more and more issues resolve themselves into one single dimension. Conversely, polarization of ideas automatically follows certain kinds of social change. Social polarization occurs as the myriad subgroups of a society are split into two conflicting camps with fewer and fewer overlapping memberships. Polarization of belief is an almost inevitable consequence of social polarization. The history of the Cold War illustrates this process nicely. It also illustrates that depolarization can occur. Now, intellectual issues seldom resolve into one great question on their own account. Intermediate positions tend not to disappear, but to multiply. Indeed, Hegel, the philosopher of intellectual history, felt they were *produced* by the interplay of extremes. The cause for polarization of belief, then, is to be sought either in social conditions, or in someone's attempt to produce social polarization.[14]

If one group can lead other groups to accept a polarized set of beliefs it can become dominant through the pervasiveness of its influence. All human activities are expressed in terms of the group's

[14]Social polarization may be brought about by polarization of belief. This is roughly Rokeach's (1968) position on race relations. It may also be brought about by social or economic causes.

goals, rather than in terms of the usual multiplicity of human goals. Consider the capitalist-communist polarity, for example. The intellectual function provided may be simplicity, but it is certainly not clarity. The social function is that of making all other groups adapt by showing either allegiance or enmity, thereby directing all organized activities into either a capitalist or a communist alliance. This general strategy is particularly effective when the opposite pole is fictitious: All activities are organized with reference to us or to nothing whatever. This too can backfire—positing a straw man can have the effect of creating a flesh and blood man to take his place.[15]

Another familiar form of polarization of belief is the stance of the small, embattled group. "He who is not with me is against me" is quite literally true of groups for which total dissolution of membership is a real threat. Such groups need members and can thrive for a time on opposition, which at least gives them relevance. Being ignored is what spells their doom. This social condition is paralleled with a set of beliefs that polarizes "us" versus everyone else, and that drives apathetics into membership or opposition.

Polarization of belief implies that the criterion of validity in any activity can be summarized in the polarizing continuum. Truth, goodness, and beauty are all aspects of capitalism versus communism, revolutionaries versus establishmentarians, or more generally, us versus them. Social identification, then, becomes the dominating criterion of validity of any kind. This is the substitution of social for intellectual criteria par excellence. It is most powerful when defined by membership in an association, the party, the church, and so forth.

SUMMARY. Beliefs persist because groups become committed to them, but for commitment to persist, the belief system must be validated. Validation is a largely social process, although the characteristics of the belief system itself, a nonsocial element, are of

[15]In what appears to be an example of this, the trial of the "Chicago Seven" for conspiracy after the 1968 Democratic convention seems to have produced exactly the conspiracy the indictment asserted had been present before the trial.

critical importance. The individual items of a belief system may be linked through a powerful logic or they may approximate a haphazard assortment linked only by tradition. They may confront disconfirming evidence from the real world or they may be couched in language that removes them from contact with the world. By cross-classifying system and empirical relevance one may describe the kinds of problems of validation generated by their own abstract characteristics, faced by belief systems, and state empirically relevant propositions concerning their ability to resist disconfirming evidence.

Validation is also a process in which commitment is maintained through the maintenance of consensus. Commitment may be viewed as varying positively with consensus and inversely with the pressure of disconfirming events.

Over and above the problems of validation produced by the abstract characteristics of belief and by problems of consensual validation, the items in a belief system are arranged according to what one may only call strategies. By strategies we do not necessarily mean to imply conscious arrangement, although this issue is moot in any number of specific cases, such as that of the "onion." Thus, the weakest link may be protected by the strongest (protecting empirically relevant beliefs by empirically nonrelevant ones, for example), or negative evidence may be shunted off through lumping and dissecting, or commitment coerced through polarizing.

Belief systems must appear to have that externality Durkheim treated so eloquently, and this chapter constructs empirically relevant propositions concerning its maintenance.

7.

Belief in Urban Society

The city is probably the single most important context for contemporary belief. By applying the theoretical orientation developed in the earlier chapters to urban social relations, we can attempt to explain the character of contemporary beliefs as well as to illustrate the orientation and, thereby, to develop its meaning. Thus the problem of this chapter is to show the consequences for belief systems of a specifically urban context.[1]

[1]If it seems that much new and apparently unrelated material is introduced in this and the next chapter, this is necessarily entailed in the application of abstract theory to any type of data. Blalock has shown that before one can connect abstract theory with actual data, another level of theory, substantive in nature, which Blalock calls

How do characteristics of beliefs facilitate their social use under peculiarly urban social conditions? What problems of validation and commitment are posed, and how are they handled in an urban environment? One typically urban approach to the problem of believability—allowing commitment in the face of the pressure of events—has already been presented: The belief system may be protected by lack of system, by lack of empirical relevance, or by a combination of the two. This and other possibilities are developed in this chapter.[2]

Urbanites adapt to the conditions of urban life both in the *character* of their beliefs and in the *mode of institutionalization* of these beliefs. The character of urban beliefs is shaped primarily by two factors: the nature of urban social integration, and the typically urban structure of social relationships. The *mode of institutionalization* refers to the secularization of belief, which can be discussed most easily as part of the process of urbanization, the topic of the next chapter. Thus we take up urban conditions in this chapter, and the process of becoming increasingly urban in the next.

THE CHARACTERISTICS OF URBANISM. The characteristics of urbanism which are of first relevance for belief systems are change, as opposed to stability; the primacy of problems in interpersonal relations over problems posed by the physical environment; and

"auxiliary" theory must be constructed (Blalock and Blalock, 1968). The new material specifies *how* the abstractions apply to the type of situation under study, which sounds obvious but generally is not. It involves a low-level, empirically based, theory of the type of situation, including many statements that are, of themselves, irrelevant to the abstract theory. For example, the law of gravity really does apply to the study of feathers in a windstorm, but in addition to the abstract law, phenomena not directly involved in gravity itself, such as wind resistance, eddy currents, and updrafts, must be studied to understand the behavior of feathers.

[2]Our discussion is dependent on a long sociological tradition including such classics as Toennies (1957), Angell (1941), Durkheim (1947), Simmel (1950), and Wirth (1938). See also Berger, Berger, and Kellner (1973), but note that they are concerned *primarily* with modernity, while we are concerned primarily with urbanism. These two concepts are less easy to distinguish than they might appear. Suffice it to say that where we focus on an abstract type of social relation, Berger and associates focus on the culture held by concrete, historically defined, societies.

institutional differentiation, as opposed to institutional homogeneity. These typically urban characteristics are produced by high population density, large populations, complex division of labor, rapid communications, and high literacy.

Urban societies have been accused of "disorganization." Although accurate on occasion, the accusation is often misleadingly documented with reference to behaviors and beliefs that have nothing to do with the integration of an urban society. In urban settings, much behavior is simply unregulated. Many actions that would be prescribed or proscribed in a folk community (and that may be prescribed within a segment of an urban society) are matters of personal freedom (to disbelieve, to drink, to stay out all night, to disobey mother) which do not interfere with the accommodative consensus (see below) or the organization of the economy, and should not be confused with societal disintegration or disorganization.

These urban liberties may lead to an anomie that has been known to incapacitate functionally important workers, yet (so far as we know) no industrial society has yet been brought to its knees by anomie. Moreover, the responses to anomie seem to be intropunitive (suicide, for example), and thus pose potentially far less societal disruption than the alternative, externally directed aggression (murder) produced by frustration in the absence of freedom. In any case, high rates of certain kinds of deviance (such as illegitimacy or desertion) that might well indicate disintegration in a folk society indicate something else in an urban society: unhappiness perhaps, or diversity, or simply the social invisibility that accompanies large, dense populations. To summarize, urban life does seem to involve egoism, individualism, anomie, and related characteristics as well as frequent deviance of certain types, but these do not necessarily spell the breakdown of social order.

THE INTEGRATION OF URBAN SOCIETY. Social diversity and rapid change threaten societal consensus and thereby the basis for consensual validation of beliefs. The consensus that integrates "traditional" societies is limited to a locale in which individuals are constantly in contact with persons with rather similar orientations and values. This fact severely limits the scale of any social organization integrated directly through common belief.

Sheer size of population also poses problems for social integration through common belief, and these problems tend to be solved differently where communications are rapid, as in urban societies. Traditional societies often present a contrasting organizational response to population size. They consist of many homogeneous local communities that are integrated from above by means of groups with their own quite distinct cultures, such as feudal aristocracies, which present different faces to the separate local communities and to their own loose organization of kinship.

Lacking bases for integration in either universal consensus or a single structure of authority, urban societies are nevertheless organizationally stable despite rapid social and cultural change. Urban centers do not come and go, nor does the character of urban "business" change greatly when the rulers change their hats or lose their heads. The integration of urban societies is based on mutual interdependence on a complex division of labor—functional integration. Diversity itself is adaptive, and this type of integration is to a degree protected by the very diversity of such societies. As long as there are many centers of power, none can become strong enough to become repressive. As long as the population is characterized by a variety of styles of participation in different belief systems and a multitude of crosscutting and overlapping memberships, the hegemony of one group is unlikely. There is, of course, a familiar demur that must be offered to this argument and we offer it below.

In spite of their organizational stability, urban societies are based on a type of social integration that is always potentially vulnerable. Mutual dependence on a complex division of labor means that the whole can be disrupted by the failure of a specialized part and that very small, highly mobilized minorities can disrupt very large organizations. The normal pattern for an urban society is stability, along with diversity and high but tolerable levels of deviance, punctuated by short periods of normative disaster. Survival depends on resilience; "business as usual" prevails the day after a riot.

Sheer consensus will not do for an urban population. When functional integration threatens to break down, as in a severe depression, or is not yet reestablished, as after a true revolution, the usual reponse is to try and replace or supplant it with normative integration, that is, integration based on consensus. After a major revolution there is typically a period in which conformity in belief (normative integration) is savagely enforced in a "reign of terror and virtue" (see Brinton, 1965:176-204). After a depression as severe as the one that overtook Weimar Germany, political appeals based on a return to normative integration attract many listeners. Nazism, with its rhetoric of race and destiny and its condemnation of "enemies," was a classic example of this. A term commonly given to this kind of normative integration is *pseudo-Gemeinschaft*. In the last analysis, however, normative integration will neither repair aircraft nor operate a city, and there is no substitute for ball bearings and garbagemen. At the moment this chapter is being finished, the urban economies of Western Europe and Japan hang precipitously on the availability of petroleum. Normative integration would be quite irrelevant if several essentially medieval Middle Eastern states were to decide that preindustrial was good enough for everyone.

Another interpretation of the conditions for stability in urban industrial society, and of their implications for belief, is generally called "mass society theory." It argues that as social organization becomes more complex, individual styles of participation become more "atomized" and culture becomes more homogeneous or standardized. Atomization refers to a state in which specialization of the individual has left each with little similarity to his neighbor, and differentiation of social organization has destroyed the layers of association (family, neighborhood, community) which protect the individual from the larger society and protect social institutions from attacks by masses of individuals temporarily mobilized by a demagogue. Mass society is said to be characterized by low levels of participation in associations (unions, political parties) and high levels of participation in more or less homogeneous beliefs:

> The main theme . . . is this: the *mass society* develops a *mass* culture in which cultural and political values and beliefs tend

> to become *homogeneous* and *fluid.* In the middle and at the bottom—in the atomized mass—people think and feel alike; but thoughts and feelings, not being firmly anchored anywhere, are susceptible to fads and fashions. At the top, poorly organized elites, themselves mass-oriented, become political and managerial manipulators, responding to short-run pressures; they fail to maintain standards and thereby encourage the spread of populism in politics, mass tastes in culture.
>
> The empirically-minded critics of such theories are impressed by the diversity of modern life. Concerning the leveling and fluidity of culture, they point to an extraordinary variety of cultural products . . . and protest that high culture has not declined but merely become more widely available. (Wilensky, 1964:175)

This argument maintains, to use a homely metaphor, that whereas culture is like a cafeteria with a large and forever increasing selection of foods, everyone chooses hamburgers and apple pie. Low levels of participation in associations and politics (that is to say social isolation or "atomization") make persons available for mobilization by demagogues on the basis of extremist belief. Extremist, in this literature, refers specifically to Communist Party or Nazi belief but may be generalized to refer to beliefs that explicitly reject procedural consensus in a society—beliefs that would ordinarily be characterized as revolutionary. Procedural consensus is discussed below.

The mass society literature developed as a response to the rise of totalitarian regimes in Europe and is specifically concerned with the dual threat to the individual and to the maintenance of democratic procedures posed by large, heterogeneous, complex, and "massified" urban societies. One of the foci of interest of the mass society writers has been on the threat to what we call *procedural consensus.* We suggest below that procedural consensus is necessary for the maintenance of social order in an urban setting.[3]

CHARACTERISTICS OF URBAN BELIEF. The conditions to which

[3]See Kornhauser (1960), Coleman (1957), and Nisbet (1953).

urban dwellers must adapt, using their beliefs (among other things), have been sketched in outline. Next, let us consider the specific nature of that adaptation, and its implications for belief in an urban context. Finally, we shall take up two crucial aspects of belief, namely commitment and validation, and relate them to urban social structure.

1. *Urban belief systems typically include two value characteristics: potency and voluntarism.* By potency we mean that urban man's general stance toward the world is one of active mastery rather than passive acceptance. Collectively, urban man *has* strongly affected (if not controlled, exactly) his physical and social environment, so that in many ways to retreat from the stance of active mastery is to retreat from urbanism. Many natural dangers have been tamed with the aid of an attitude toward disease, flood, earthquake, and climate that would be taken as sheer hubris in a folk society. The same stance, regardless of its justification, is often adopted in relation to social organization. Many Americans feel that the War on Poverty, for example, *was* sheer hubris.

Without this attitude of potency, voluntarism would be meaningless. What would it mean to accord individuals the right and obligation to choose, if their choices were perceived to have no influence on events? In fact, this very dilemma is the taproot of that phenomenon called *anomie* by contemporary sociologists (Merton, 1949). The most consistent empirical correlate of anomie as a measured attitude is low social status, a position in which one is encouraged to choose things that he cannot, in fact, attain.

As presented by Toennies (1957), but much neglected since, voluntarism is central in the way urbanites view the relations among humans, and between humans and the natural environment.

Let us focus for a moment on the individual rather than on social structure or systems of belief. Voluntarism poses the urban dweller with special problems in using his beliefs to adapt to social conditions on the vicissitudes of his personal life. That *some* problem exists is recognized not only in academic literature but in the popular press as well. One way of viewing this problem would have it that a "permanent identity crisis" exists, which is caused by the fact that urban people have many alternative identities available to them, are always planning far ahead in relation to these identities, are always subject to change, and are responsive to the ways other people react (Berger et al., 1973).

We prefer a different way of viewing this situation. We suspect that this "crisis" has less to do with "identity" than with voluntarism as a value deeply set in urban belief. It is not merely the case that statuses are no longer comfortably ascribed; to a very considerable degree, important statuses *are* ascribed, as 20 or more years of research on sex roles and on occupational aspirations clearly demonstrates.

The "crisis," if any, stems from conflict between the imperative to choose one's own identity, and the practical difficulty in doing so; or the conflict between what one wants to be and what one thinks one *ought* to be.

2. *Urban beliefs parallel urban social structure. They are diverse, heterogeneous, and subject to change.* Elaborate and incompatible systems of belief coexist, avoiding conflict by means of specialization and compartmentalized thought, while much belief, like much behavior, is unregulated. In belief as well as social structure, urban life therefore appears to be at once regimented and disorganized. Belief, like social interaction, is segmentalized, universalistic, dispassionate, and individualistic in the public arena, elthough it may be quite the reverse within private social settings. The consequence of such a congery of beliefs is similar to the consequence of urban social structure: it contains conflict and fosters a complex division of labor. Both adapt to demographic size, density, and heterogeneity, as well as to rapid social change. In short, much of the character of modern belief (secularization, variety, transitoriness, and so on) is to be explained as a direct consequence of the single dominant social context of belief in industrial countries, namely urban social organization.

Where the technology not only changes, but also permits ever greater control over the natural environment, the empirical relevance of many beliefs declines. We elevate goals, values, and central beliefs to the realm of the nonempirical both to protect them from invalidation and to reduce their rate of change. Beliefs once solidly based on the daily experiences of the average man, such as the solidity of matter, the flatness of the earth, the constancy of gravity, and the identity of mass and weight, are contradicted in the daily lives not only of esoteric specialists but of general followers of the news as well. Urbanites have become accustomed to the rapid adjustments in such beliefs that follow when science *leads* technology and new techniques are quickly put into practice.

3. *The problems to which urban beliefs are addressed are the problems of urban people.* Urban beliefs are quite typically concerned with either interpersonal relationships, inner peace, or with individual potency of some kind. This is not a recent phenomenon, although massive shifts of population to urban centers in recent years emphasize it. Weber observed that one of the appeals of Christianity to the artisan class of second or third century Rome was its emphasis on personal reliability. The vast layer of manipulative beliefs and folklore concerning health, avoidance of natural disasters, weather, and so forth characteristic of so much human history has, to a considerable degree, disappeared and has been replaced with movements such as New Light that deal with general potency or success in interpersonal relationships.

Through the 1930s in the United States, a rather large number of small urban belief systems developed that emphasized the development of personal competence through learning esoteric dogmas that were a melange of Eastern philosophy and Christianity. The war years (1941-1945) saw an apparent diminution of this kind of belief and the late 1960s has seen a massive popular revival of interest in meditation, astrology, the occult, divination, and many variants on the Buddhist theme (Clark, 1949; Braden, 1949). Post-World War II Japan has witnessed a religious revival of major political importance in which the content of the beliefs seems to concern the achievement of personal goals (McFarland, 1967). "Peace of mind" in its many variants, both religious and secular, is concerned with personal competence "in trying times" and is only vaguely related to the intense concern with salvation characteristic of preurban

Europe and America. In a not too different vein, Father Divine, a most urban prophet, concerned himself deeply with interpersonal relations. Much of the specific normative system of his Peace Mission Movement regulated interpersonal conduct (Braden, 1949). Very recently, belief systems such as Arica, Transcendental Meditation, Scientology, and Dianetics, which are classic examples of the urban type just described, have become big business in the most literal sense.

The simplest explanation of the enormous success of yoga and of the following gathered by various gurus, as well as the fact that two forms of meditation are now sold exactly as other material commodities are, is that these are perfect urban belief systems directed toward self-realization, escape from tension (specifically Transcendental Meditation in this case), and smoothing interpersonal relationships. One other characteristic of these belief systems, their total apoliticality, may either be a *response* to the political disappointments of 1960-1972 or may *foreshadow* a generalized retreat from empirically relevant belief.

This kind of switch away from avoiding natural disasters and toward developing personal competence and guaranteeing good interpersonal relations simply reflects the adaptive characteristic of belief. If we were somehow to return to the conditions of Cro-Magnon life, Transcendental Meditation would probably be eclipsed by weather magic of some kind. Urban beliefs reflect urban problems.

4. *In urban settings, procedural consensus replaces substantive consensus.* Under urban conditions, *homogeneity* of belief cannot provide the basis for orderly social life because the variety and specialization of urban populations destroy the structural basis (similarity) on which homogeneity of belief might be based. Deviance cannot be defined in terms of difference, as it often is by nonurban people, but must be seen as a disruption of the social order as defined by law and by the norms governing economic interdependence. Urban societies, of course, depend on consensus of certain types and in some degree. Indeed, the existence of institutions adapted to any social context implies a measure of

consensus. But since the interdependence itself provides integration, full consensus of belief is not necessary for that purpose. Thus, although consensus on substantive beliefs is neither necessary nor possible, *procedural consensus* is crucial. That is, we need not all believe the same thing but it is absolutely necessary that we agree upon some minimum set of procedures for adjudicating differences. Consensus on substance is characteristic of a cult within urban or rural society. Consensus on procedures for adjudicating differences is characteristic, and necessary, for the operation of a complex society integrated on the basis of functional interdependence. Much attention has been paid by political sociologists to the problem of maintaining and protecting such procedural consensus.

In the short run, even consensus on procedures may be absent without jeopardizing social order if "pluralistic ignorance" exists. Pluralistic ignorance is the condition in which groups of people perceive substantive agreement in belief specifically because they misunderstand one another and each projects his own beliefs onto the others. This may allow a population to live in peaceful disharmony for what seems to be an indefinite period of time, engaging in occasional rituals that emphasize consensus and that are either so low in empirical relevance and so well established in tradition that they do not bear on current conflicts of belief, or so vague and platitudinous that they are almost without specific content. We will comment below on the applicability of this generalization.

Simmel (1955) once observed that ritual is a means of producing cohesion where other means are lacking. By this he meant that in heterogeneous populations where a high degree of differentiation exists in life-style and hence beliefs, some cohesion may be produced by ritual (a form of procedural consensus) alone. Ritual is fundamentally harmless. Although you can be fairly sure that some United States senators dislike the ritual involved in opening the Senate, no one speaks out. Religious ritual is typically far removed from empirical reality; the more heterogeneous the population served by a religious group the more ritualized the services are likely to be. National churches such as the Church of England have typically used ritual very heavily. The sect, on the other hand, has less need for ritual—it has, or can enforce, substantive consensus. As generations pass and the original consensus breaks down, ritual begins to appear at first only in an "order of business," but later in the use of vestments and visual symbols. A more or less typical history of a social movement can be written in terms of the erosion of substantive consensus and its replacement by ritual, rules for conducting business, and so forth.

Overarching political rituals are typically vague, probably deliberately so. Until recently the Democratic Party in the United States was composed of Eastern welfare-state oriented liberals and Southern white populists. Its programs and policies were so hedged about with evasions and qualifications and its platforms couched in such grandiose and empty language that a little pluralistic ignorance permitted the association of incompatible beliefs. "The American Way," "The Fatherland," "Our Queen" are very useful slogans where there is little other ground for agreement. The point made above is crucial to the understanding of the institutionalization of beliefs. To a considerable degree, institutionalization is a process in which procedural consensus is substituted for substantive consensus.

When groups interact they are apt to come to understand one another, and this makes pluralistic ignorance an unstable basis for integration. It usually topples only when some (possibly irrelevant) social issue forces open channels of communication that are "normally" closed, thus introducing a new social problem, namely the reestablishment of social order on a rather more difficult basis. In the case of the Democratic Party, the Indochina war and responses of Americans to it have destroyed pluralistic ignorance, possibly beyond repair. Nevertheless, pluralistic ignorance is not to be underrated as a basis for urban social integration.

5. *The beliefs associated with the organization of an urban society as a whole involve an accommodative consensus on how to live and let live.* This should be true even in totalitarian societies that permit only a narrow range of belief. Urban societies consist of structures within which there may be homogeneity, but between

which the underlying stratum of consensus is only on a set of procedures which foster accommodation. Accommodation is sufficient for many purposes, although some activities require coordination.

The intricate coordination characteristic of many aspects of urban life is achieved either within formal bureaucratic structures that elaborate procedure in minute detail, or it results from a market mechanism, only the outlines of which need to be agreed on. Changes in the conditions surrounding both accommodation and coordination, of course, continually occur as shifts between these two types of structural adaptation. Thus, when a market mechanism has intolerable consequences an increasingly bureaucratic framework is negotiated to replace or modify it. When a bureaucratic framework of rules becomes irrelevant or unworkable by virtue of its own cost or complexity, market mechanisms emerge willy-nilly.

Such a basis for social integration leads apologists of a traditional social order to see, in urbanism, the destruction not only of specific values (honesty, thrift, godliness, morality, respect for elders, and so forth), but of social organization itself. In the sense that the new problems of human organization generated by urbanism cannot be solved on the basis of a type of consensus that no longer exists, such apologists are correct. As shown by Durkheim in *The Division of Labor* (1947), however, homogeneity is not the only possible basis for the societal integration. Apart from the accommodative consensus, integration is not accomplished by single-mindedness and unity in an urban society, but through specialized institutional arrangements (such as the judiciary) and through the dependence of all on a complex division of labor. In fact, the type of belief system which promotes solidarity in a small primitive tribe would be useless in an urban society. The amount of culture people *can* hold in common is probably much too limited to organize the variety of activities performed in an urban society.

Surprisingly, urban societies show particularly strong organizational stability. It is not based on widespread substantive agreement. Apart from a substantial shared knowledge, the urban consensus could be described as an enormous number of people who share a comparatively small number of substantive beliefs. Many of those ("We are the greatest nation on earth," for example) are shared, and useful in integration, only to the extent that they are vague or ambiguous. The complex and productive economy, however, and the set of highly developed institutions (law, education, medicine, police, the military, and so on) are largely responsible for the organizational stability. Depending upon the particular society, mass communications play a role as important, possibly, as all the other institutions taken together.

If these remarks on the nature of urban social life and its implications for belief are true, then commitment would seem almost impossible to maintain under urban conditions. Indeed, though commitment is a problem under all conditions, such considerations have led many writers to identify urbanism and modernity with disbelief. This is to assume that commitment defines belief, however, and we have taken commitment as a variable characteristic of belief.

COMMITMENT AND URBAN BELIEF. With some exceptions, urban beliefs generally do not demand absolute commitment. The dichotomous choice between total commitment and apostasy more often occurs under one of the following sets of conditions.

1. A folk society in which the entire population belongs to the cult and in which belief and membership are synonymous.
2. A small dissident association in an urban environment that is faced with rejection, illegality, or some other dire external threat. The association need not be religious; it could be an outlaw motorcycle gang or a revolutionary party.
3. A religious institution highly identified with the political process in a society that is subject to external threat. This is one of the explanations for the extraordinary emphasis on religious conformity in seventeenth century England and, possibly, also for the rather considerable heat generated in twentieth century America by the hip life-style. As in the preurban village, some degree of

superficial conformity is demanded to keep one from being branded as an enemy or outsider.

Skepticism is practically a requirement for survival in urban society. Not only experiences with technological and societal change, but also personal changes of social position involving identification and therefore belief (such as job mobility or marriage) motivate tentativeness of commitment. To be gullible in an urban society is to invite the manipulations of every kind of charlatan from confidence man to auto mechanic. Since commitment is a means for social manipulation, and since manipulation is the law of the urban jungle, urbanites develop the skill of protecting themselves from the consequences of their own commitments.

Skepticism is a general stance, but compartmentalization leaves areas of uncritical belief, nevertheless. Folk tales about the city boy and his country cousin paint the city boy as just as gullible regarding the reproductive behavior of farm animals as the hick is concerning urban transportation. They are equally *ignorant,* but the gullibility of each depends on the kind of trust he places in given social relationships. The country boy is unfamiliar with secondary relationships, and therefore does not expect to be lied to as a matter of course. Even city dwellers who under no circumstances would buy shares in the Brooklyn Bridge or flee the city after an apparent radio announcement of Martian invasion are nevertheless regularly open to two kinds of uncritical belief: (1) unquestioned assumptions, which they probably do not recognize as belief (for example, in the availability of clean water from a kitchen tap), and (2) certain specialized areas where the source of information is limited and the source of the belief is a primary relationship. The popularity of several blatantly fraudulent gurus among otherwise sophisticated and skeptical urban students may be explained this way.

The time and space perspectives of urban belief systems are apt to be extremely broad, but intense commitment may be restricted to a very narrow band of time or even to a very small segment of the persons' interests. Fads typically sweep through urban areas and are replaced by still other fads to which believers give a high level of rather temporary commitment. Unlike the condition of the peasant society, in which tradition is a major basis for legitimacy and in which the duration of a belief is the measure of its strength, urban dwellers may exhibit intense temporary commitments because there is no necessary implication of duration, or because logical connections between belief systems are not made clear. Thus intense belief in reincarnation can be kept from interfering with one's occupation as a physician. One may be a devout spiritualist today and a devout atheist tomorrow—a useful adaptation in a world of rapid change in technology and intergroup relations.

The set of beliefs held by an individual, though each belief comes from a logically developed system, may not hold implications for one another, that is they may be an unsystematic set. For example, the set might be $E = MC^2$, cross only on the green light, and used car salesmen are unreliable. This is to say that an individual's belief parallels his social relations, which are characterized by great functional specificity.[4]

VALIDATION AND URBAN BELIEF. *The validity of beliefs in urban settings is protected by institutional differentiation.* One can speak of *the* belief system of a society only in the case of undifferentiated folk societies, in which the community of believers is coextensive with the population. As institutional differentiation occurs, one or more new special purpose associations will emerge to organize the relevant activity. To the extent that each consists of

[4]Under the term *pluralization of life-worlds,* this lack of system has been held largely responsible for the "permanent identity crisis" afflicting modern man by Berger, Berger, and Kellner (1973). We take it, on the contrary, as an adaptation to social conditions: as a *solution* to the problem of identity that would face modern man if he tried to order his beliefs after the fashion of an Australian aborigine. Personal identities, we hold, are socially constructed out of interaction with other people, as outlined by George Herbert Mead in *Mind, Self, and Society.* Only professional intellectuals form identities out of the interplay of ideas. Thus, insofar as there is conflict in the attempt to relate the various parts of self, it is because of the complexity of social relations, not the complexity of beliefs.

In coming to terms with complex social relations, individuals of course employ a wide variety of types of belief, and the characteristics of each type determine how

an independent network of communication, it may be expected to develop an independent belief system with its own inner logic. In the highly urban situation, there are multitudes of such belief systems which free the individual from full reliance on any one of them, and enhance the possibility of not taking any one of them very seriously.[5]

The structure of an urban society is not the same as the structure of its component parts, and the parts, of course, differ radically among themselves. This is as true of beliefs as it is of the social structures which carry them. The social diversity of urban society is paralleled by a truly bewildering diversity of beliefs. Contrasting belief systems, contained in intricately related—even overlapping—social structures, differ not only in content but in all the variable characteristics, of belief outlined in Chapter 2. The parts of an urban society may range from true gemeinschafts to units that are themselves internally complex. Beliefs, then, may run the same gamut.

The simple connection between social structure and belief established in the folk society is replaced with a complex connection in the urban society. The membership of a cult may be very small in relation to the size of the community of believers (see the discussion of social organization in Chapter 4). In the extreme case, the cult may disappear altogether, for a time at least. This has been the case with anti-Semitism for some hundreds of years. It has retained a community of believers of variable size but has been consciously elaborated by a cult only in periods of economic and political crisis, as in late Czarist Russia, Weimar and Nazi Germany, and Know-Nothing and Great Depression America.

well or ill the type is fit to the task to which it is put. One may do a bad job with a good tool, or a good job with a bad tool, so that there is no *deterministic* connection between characteristics of the tool and the success of the enterprise: integration of the parts of self, in this case. The reader can probably think of *individuals* who achieve more or less integrated personalities with the help of all sorts of ideological tools. But we would suggest that some (a cosmic harmony *Weltanschauung* such as that of Dr. Pangloss in *Candide*, for example) are rather awkward for the purpose of contending with personal problems engendered by complex social relations. Under urban conditions, cosmic harmony is akin to the defense mechanism known as denial.

[5]See for examples Braden (1949, 1963) and Cantril (1941).

The process of validation, therefore, is greatly complicated by urban conditions. Thus while some beliefs are firmly tied to an ongoing system, others become more or less unmoored from a social context to guide their interpretation. What is the significance of kissing one's sister under the mistletoe? There is no possibility of an authoritative answer, unless one accepts such reconstituted Druidical societies as exist in England as being able to *recreate* doctrine. In the absence of written documents as well as historical continuity, the legitimacy of interpretation is up for grabs.

The existence of beliefs that have unclear criteria of validity is not necessarily a result of the above sort of historical process, as we show in the next chapter. There are always free-floating, relatively unattached beliefs available in urban populations that lack this history of a legitimating cult. The invention and development of the institution of Mother's Day in the United States is probably a case in point. Every year the Sunday supplements carry attempts to invent the equivalent of a validating cult in history, but the significant point is not the imputed desire for a legitimatizing cult; it is the fact that urbanites are accustomed to such ambiguities, whether they result from historical processes or from recent inventions. Under nonurban social conditions, ambiguity in the process of legitimate validation would be settled immediately by group membership but the fact of multiple, overlapping group memberships in urban societies often means that the issue of legitimate validation is allowed simply to hang, unresolved.

VALIDITY, COMMITMENT, AND URBAN SOCIAL STRUCTURE. Relations *between* urban structures differ from relations *within* them. Urban beliefs carried by specialized institutional structures may be highly systematic, but the multitude of systems is protected by functional specificity (the social system analogue of compartmentalized thought in the individual). Thus the mutual implications of cosmology, social ethics, and biblical scholarship tend to be asserted less and less strongly as each enterprise is itself developed in an increasingly systematic way.

Denying systematic linkages between certain ideas allows us to deny the possibility of contradiction, permitting that peculiarly urban form of syncretism which sees remarkably diverse collections of belief as all true, as all manifestations of the same underlying reality. This type of segmentation protects validity and prevents social as well as intellectual conflict. The fundamentalist laboratory technician, for example, parades the compatibility of his occupational and religious knowledge in public, but his personal mechanism of adjusting the two is most often compartmentalization. Religion and science cannot conflict *in principle* for him, because if they did, it would imply either that he is accepting money under false pretenses or that his marriage is invalid, and since both of these theorems are incorrect, the premise must be rejected. The doctrines of each institution are experienced separately and, within their own context, each seems entirely reasonable. The necessary appearance of externality is maintained by segregation of potentially conflicting beliefs.

Within segments of urban societies, however, consensus and commitment may be very high indeed; higher, in fact, than is possible in folk or feudal societies, because within such segments there may be far greater social homogeneity than could possibly occur within a societal structure faced by all the problems of existence. A complex society, through specialization, frees certain segments from important social contacts with divergent social perspectives. Within such groups, it is possible to interact on the basis of norms and of substantive beliefs, and to allow other elements of the belief system—ultimate goals, system logic, criteria of validity, and orientation—to remain implicit: they are well understood by all, and unquestionable in any case. *Between* such homogeneous groups, however, interaction tends to take place by making values, logic, orientation, and criteria of validity explicit and taking them as bones of contention.

Because of these homogeneous enclaves, collectivism as well as individualism is fostered by the urban environment. Neither, of course, is really an issue in traditional society. Urbanism fosters individualism by distinguishing between the interests of an individual and those of his family or town. It fosters collectivism by producing collections of other individuals whose interests are more similar to one's own than could be possible in a traditional society. Both Karl Marx and Ralph Waldo Emerson were addressing specifically urban conditions, and it is hard to see how either could have been produced in a feudal social structure. Thus urbanism has an effect on the content, as well as the form, of urban belief.

SUMMARY. The city is the most important social context of contemporary Western belief. Its consequences for belief are profound and are due to the characteristics of urban life itself.

Urban belief adapts to urban social organization. Differentiation and specialization in one reflect differentiation and specialization in the other. Substantive consensus is lacking and probably impossible except for short periods of time and within specalized oroups of people in urban society, but the maintenance of socal order requires some agreement on procedures, and some agreement to live and let live.

Urban belief systems quite typically deal with the problems of urban people—interpersonal relations and intrapersonal competence. The elements of urban belief systems are likely to be worked out in some detail and made explicit.

High commitment is not usually a demand of urban belief—skepticism is more common—but the very complexity that feeds skepticism also makes possible homogeneous associations within which consensus may be higher than could possibly be achieved in any preurban settlement.

8.

Urbanization and Belief

The process of becoming increasingly urban includes the whole spectrum of social change, from basic demographic alterations to growing reliance on the mass media. Rather than describing urbanization as a total process, however, we abstract a few changes in social organization for special attention. Such abstraction is necessary if we are to consider the sociology of urbanization, as distinct from simply explaining the intellectual history of certain urbanizing populations of European extraction. Furthermore, the changes listed below have special implications for systems of belief.

As they urbanize, societies experience an enormous increase in the structural complexity of all institutions except the kinship system. This striking change occurs as organizations, collections of activities, and beliefs that are already institutionalized become still further differentiated and reorganized. During this process, functions are removed from some structures and new structures are established for their perpetuation, and so on ad infinitum. Thus, popular entertainment and education have both been differentiated from the family and established in more specialized institutions of their own which have, in turn, become still further specialized. At the same time that institutional differentiation takes place, however, more and more of life is relegated to a residual category not covered by any organization or institution. This process, which involves simultaneous specialization and "massification," and its consequences for belief, is the topic of this chapter.

We observe four interrelated processes that occur during urbanization.

1. Massification and bureaucratization, in which urban social structure comes to be dominated by large populations with few tight communal bonds, and by large, highly organized, highly specialized concerns.
2. Secularization, which is a consequence of differentiation and which we define as a process in which belief systems become unmoored from the institutions that originally carried them. This somewhat unusual use of this term is discussed further on in the chapter.
3. Differentiation, in which several more focused institutions replace one larger one. In this process there is a decrease in the franchise of the more specialized institutions to explain, regulate, and justify aspects of life.
4. The growth of new belief systems suited to the social vehicles available in the massified areas of urban society.

The process of institutional differentiation itself is an interesting and traditional topic in sociology, but our aim is to emphasize more specifically what happens to *systems of belief* as institutions differentiate.[1] If a system is a collection of things (beliefs in this case) which are mutually related to one another, and one of those things changes, then one ought generally to expect adjustments in the related things, a decline in the interrelatedness of the system, or a little of both. That is, social change poses special threats to the extent of commitment, the traditional process of validation, and the extent of system in existing belief systems.

The adaptations to change manifested in the beliefs of individual members of changing societies are complex. First, the adaptation of the belief system itself may differ from the adaptation of an individual believer. For a brief example, a religious belief system facing validity threats from the pressure of events might adapt by becoming empirically less relevant, while an individual believer (who also holds portions of other types of belief systems) might adapt by compartmentalizing his Sundays. Second, the adaptations often take place both in the relation between the ideas—the extent and nature of the system—as well as in the content of the ideas. But content may have relevance for system, producing further complexity. For example, an urban minister's action program in changing neighborhoods based on the "love thy neighbor" theme can raise questions on how "love thy neighbor" is related to other points of doctrine and convention in a novel and poignant way.

Among the examples and applications of beliefs responding to specific changes associated with urbanization given below, some will be instances of beliefs which are not clearly tied to any system at all, and some are apparently tied to several different systems of belief at once. The point is not that such ambiguity is necessarily produced in the history of a specific idea, but that the typical history of belief systems through urbanization produces a great deal of ambiguity with which urbanites must learn to live. Accustomed to this type of ambiguity, urbanites *produce* relatively isolated beliefs

[1]The changing functions of various institutionalized structures, along with differentiation, has long been an important point of theoretical departure for sociologists attempting to explain current social changes. See, for example, Park (1952), Chapin (1935), or Burgess (1948). The general approach to societal differentiation has been summarized and developed in Parsons (1961) and Smelser (1957). For an example of these materials applied to the current American religious scene, see Parsons (1960).

that have no histories at all, and they may even invent histories for them. Advertising agencies find this kind of activity quite profitable.

MASSIFICATION AND BUREAUCRATIZATION. Urbanization is traditionally seen as consisting of the development of "mass" society characterized by large numbers of different kinds of people living in close physical proximity without either a tight network of interpersonal relationships or a common culture. *Atomization,* implying the destruction of common bonds, both of interaction and belief, is the term most often used to describe the character of personal life. Toennies, Simmel, Wirth, and others have described the breakdown of a single overarching moral order and the complex primary group network which perpetuates it, leaving the impression that the urban man is socially isolated in an unorganized mass of others.[2] Urban social relations are characterized as mediated largely through ecological processes; that is, people and activities are organized through mutual dependence rather than socal interaction. The great dichotomies such as mechanical-organic, sacred-secular, and ideational-sensate that have been so prominent in the history of sociology all reflect concern with this general model of urbanization. Cultural diversity, according to this view, is accounted for by the existence of the mass media, which present the same stimuli to large numbers of individuals outside of the context of social interaction. The resulting "mass culture," based on the standardization of culture, does not presume very much about the socialization experiences of its participants, except insofar as mass education permits the possibility of a somewhat more sophisticated mass culture.

The mass, as a type of social organization, is identified by its extreme simplicity, which is not to say its lack of organization. Blumer (1946) distinguishes the mass by four characteristics: (1)

[2]See the early work of Ferdinand Toennies (1957), Simmel (1950), and the more recent adaptation of these materials in Wirth (1938). This view has much to recommend it as a picture of *some* aspects of the process of urbanization for certain population segments. Uncritically generalized to whole cities, however, it is grossly incorrect—see Janowitz (1952), and Young and Willmott (1957).

social heterogeneity in all respects except that the members are all oriented to or subject to some issue, event, or social condition, (2) the anonymity of its members, (3) relative lack of interaction or even contact among most of the members, and (4) looseness of organization, that is, disunity or lack of ability to take concerted and coordinated action. A society that exhibits mass organization is in fact internally differentiated according to social class, ethnic group, age, region, sex, and other categories, and is composed of persons who interact in families, cliques, and so on, but it constitutes only an extremely loose network of communication. Given these simple principles of organization, the number of members is so large *in relation to the number of different social positions* that, for the purposes of acting on a specific issue, the mass may be regarded as relatively undifferentiated. This is not, however, to attribute the character of a mob to modern society. If one conceives of folk or peasant societies as the normal condition of mankind and urban societies as deviations from that norm, it seems to be possible to regard any form of mass organization as social *dis*organization, moral corruption, or worse. Edward Shils has paraphrased what he considers to be the most pessimistic view of mass society:

> Power is concentrated in this society, and much of the power takes the form of manipulation of the mass through the media of mass communication. Civic spirit is poor, local loyalties are few, primordial solidarity is virtually non-existent. There is no individuality, only a restless and frustrated egoism. It is like the state of nature described by Thomas Hobbes, except that public disorder is restrained through the manipulation of the elite and the apathetic idiocy of the mass. The latter is broken only when, in a state of crisis, the masses rally around some demagogue. (1962:45-47).

Shils, however, regards this image as inapplicable to urban society, the assumed causal relationships not in fact supported by the available evidence, and the value imputations open to serious questions. Rather, as he points out, elements of mass organization on a large scale are relatively novel in human history, and have most frequently occurred when supported by a novel type of normative order. This chapter attempts to state the implications of a mass form of social organization for such a normative system. But before we can do this, we should complement this view of urban society with another.

An apparently competing view of urbanization rests on the assumption that bureaucracies are becoming the dominant form of organization of social structures in all institutional areas. Corporations, governments, churches, universities, and so on are becoming more centralized and internally more highly specialized. The urban man described by Weber, Riesman, Whyte, Miller, Swanson, and others seems to be an administrative official who divides his leisure time among a host of formal organizations all devoted to the efficient service of some specialized end.[3] The problems set by nature would seem to have all been solved; all that remains is the problem of human administration, the coordination and control of vast numbers of technical experts. Cultural diversity, according to this view, is accounted for by specialization; uniformity, by the concept of bureaucratic conformity.

As a type of social organization, bureaucracy is at the opposite pole from the mass type of organization. It occurs in response to great administrative complexity and extreme differentiation. How can the activities of large numbers of specialists be organized and coordinated in pursuit of a common goal? The number of differentiated but coordinated social categories is high in relation to the number of people, and the sheer number of administrative tasks necessitates the development of some set of procedures to handle them.

Organizational response to extreme differentiation usually entails formal rules, written records, systems of recruitment and socialization, regular careers, administrative offices, bodies of esoteric knowledge, and so on. This response is not restricted to government or the organization of production, but appears in all the different types of organized activities that are carried out in a social context.

[3]Weber's significant discussions on bureaucratic organization are dispersed among his writings, but see especially Gerth and Mills (1958:196-266). Also see Riesman et el., (1950), Whyte (1957), and Miller and Swanson (1958).

As societies become more urban, all of the institutionalized activities such as socialization of the young, defense against foreign powers, maintenance of public safety, production, the allocation of goods and services, technical knowledge, art, religion, and entertainment become more highly differentiated and hence separated from one another. It is within these various clusters of organized, large-scale activities that bureaucracy arises.

These two contrasting images of urban social organization do not contradict one another, but describe different aspects of the same modern urban reality. Folk or peasant societies exhibit neither mass nor bureaucratic organization to any marked degree; urban societies exhibit both. Increasing institutional differentation produces the increasingly bureaucratic organization of the structures which implement institutions and of the development of a bureaucratic structure encompassing the entire society. But it also forces the society as a whole to exhibit a mass form of organization with respect to a great range of social activities. The two views of urban society are not only compatible but mutually dependent.

The fact that urban social organization was becoming both mass and bureaucratic in character, and that both trends were occurring for the same reason—specialization—was observed by sociologists long before society reached its present complexity. The existence of a mass public with regard to general issues, that often exhibits a complex organization on highly specific issues is a commonplace fact of current American political life. Such a possibility was the basis for Weber's remark that "the great state and the mass party are the classic soil for bureaucratization" (Gerth and Mills, 1958:209). Durkheim's description of urbanization suggests that as a single moral order crumbles before the myriad differences between men engendered by specialization; other associations (based on the similarities between men within the same speciality) grow up to mediate in the relation between the individual and his society.[4] Yet

[4]We are referring here to what Berger, Berger, and Kellner (1973) call "multi-relational synchronization." Their whole discussion is directly relevant here, since *at this point* we too are discussing the individual's predicament as he confronts a changing social context for belief.

this mediation is necessarily incomplete. If specialization makes men different, it also isolates men, leaving them similarly helpless and dependent when unspecialized issues arise.

These two contrasting forms of social organization, the mass and the bureaucracy, meet in the life of the individual. One may work for a corporation, educate his children in a school system, worship in a church, belong to a union, continue his reserve status in the army, act as an officer in an international stamp collecting association, do volunteer work for a political party, and still find himself an insignificant part of an undifferentiated mass at election time trying to solve an obviously complex issue with a dichotomous vote on the basis of the meager information available in the mass media. Working in a bureaucracy, yet subject to the mass media during leisure hours, each individual finds that he has a great deal in common with very few others and a little in common with a vast number of others. Those areas in which he has little in common with others, that is those in which he and the others are organized as a mass, are the arenas in which he must make decisions with full authority and responsibility as an individual. In his daily life, then, an individual moves among many different bureaucratic structures. Because there are so many such individuals, and because the bureaucracies among which they move make their interests so different that they have only very simple elements in common, they are organized as a mass.

In the attempt to integrate his life experiences within the context of many different bureaucracies, the individual is alone and unaided, like the myriad of others in the same predicament.[5] Since his life is not totally committed to any one of the institutional areas within which bureaucracies arise (and between which there exists a bureaucratic structure at the societal level), such a person finds that the integration of the various aspects of his life is necessarily an individual or family matter. There are few other *general* social

[5]On loss of religious basis, the traditional terminology leads Berger, Berger, and Kellner (1973) to assert that "pluralization of life-worlds" produces secularization, whereas, in our terminology, secularization is one basic process through which "plural life-worlds" arise.

relationships. Even interaction with neighbors, friends, and distant relatives tends to be circumscribed by a limited range of mutual or appropriate interests. Specialists armed with highly developed bodies of knowledge are available with presumably excellent advice regarding many specific aspects of life, but none can tell an individual how to behave. In normative terms, they have neither the *right* nor the *competence.*

In summary, societies characterized by bureaucratic organization within the major institutional areas also tend to develop bureaucratic superstructures, yet the organization of much of the remaining structure in such societies is not bureaucratic but mass in type. Institutional differentiation produces mass organization at the societal level for two reasons. First, as the various specialties become more highly differentiated, areas not covered by *any* specific specialty emerge. Second, the problem of integrating all the specialties is far too great for even a bureaucratic form of organization. A mass results. One organizational response to size and complexity, in other words, is an administrative superstructure that regulates the relations among the specialties and allocates spheres of authority and competence. In the vast realms of behavior not directly coordinated by such a superstructure, the many differences between individuals are not integrated through complementarity of function because a complex division of labor is effective only in relation to the specific tasks that constitute the "labor that was divided," and specialties merely constitute differences in relation to other tasks. It is the similarities between individuals, not the differences, that contribute to the integration of these individuals in collective action.

Each individual is like each other individual in relation to that action, and the likeness is based on the small area of culture which all the specialized individuals have in common. Modern urban societies are bureaucratic in some areas and mass in others, and an increase in the extent of one type of organization is likely to be paralleled by increases in the other.

Thus mass *and* bureaucratic organization of urban societies is the social precondition for secularization, as defined later in this chapter. *Secular beliefs are developed and perpetuated through the mass form of organization.* Novel ideas about health may have originated in clinics, just as novel ideas about God may have originated in seminaries, and those about nutrition in laboratories, but the practical belief systems that come to contain these ideas are not developed and perpetuated within the bureaucratic institutional structures so much as in the uninstitutionalized mass. Because the "inner sanctum" of a complex institution is readily accessible to so few, and because it may deal with areas of belief important to all of us, the secularization of belief is an important and inevitable concomitant of urbanization.

SECULARIZATION OF BELIEF. Let us borrow the term *secularization* from the specifically religious context in which it most commonly appears and give it a meaning with a more general referent in social structure. Although the term is usually used to refer to the shrinking franchise of organized religious belief, it actually describes a process that occurs to *all* institutions as they differentiate and specialize. We use it in this more general sense. Secularization is *the separation of a belief system from the relatively bureaucratic institutional structure within any institutional area.* The continued existence of a belief system must be explained by *some* social structure; when the social support for a belief becomes a mass type of organization rather than an association, the belief has become secular.

Thus, this use of the term *secular* does not mean that the beliefs in question do not motivate commitment, but rather that they have been removed from their original institutional source, and whatever validation they acquire and commitment they are able to generate have sources other than the original institution. You probably believe in the existence of germs, for example, and in their association with dirt. You wash things to escape illness. But you did not learn these beliefs from physicians or microbiologists (who hold rather different beliefs about germs, dirt, and illness), you learned them from your mother and have had them validated by your friends and neighbors. These are now secular beliefs.

Traditionally, secularization has referred to the removal of a belief from the domain of churches, whatever its later fate (Durkheim, 1947). Borrowing the term underlines our first point, namely the similarity in social structure between trends in religion and in other urban institutions. In all areas, complex and systematic belief systems are developed by professionals, but at the same time individuals live by less elaborate belief systems maintained through the nonbureaucratic network of interpersonal relations.

Some beliefs once sanctioned by religion are simply shifted over into other institutional structures such as science, government, and education. This is a change in the mode of institutionalization. Other beliefs no longer derive their social support from churches, but have not established a foothold in the bureaucratic structure within any other institutional area. Some beliefs regarding sickness and health are not grounded in the institution of medicine, not all beliefs regarding the physical world are grounded in science, some beliefs regarding the legitimate loci of power are not grounded in the constitution, and so on.

We must distinguish between a process in which beliefs *become* secularized and one in which beliefs *arise afresh* in the relatively uninstitutionalized areas of life. Failure to make this distinction would ignore most of what is known about the processes of innovation and selection in social movements, and would involve us in a semantic horror, to wit: a belief system that was highly sacred in character and that arose in such a massified erea of society would have to be described as secularized. It is, of course, in these massified areas that new belief systems arise. Examples are the neosacral movements such as occultism, Eastern religions, yoga, and meditation in the United States, and the new religions of Japan (Tiryakian, 1972; Thomsen, 1963). Both processes characterize urban societies, the secularization of belief, and the rise of new institutions and their associated belief systems.

Used in this way, the statement that *urbanization produces secularization of belief through institutional differentiation* becomes a very general hypothesis in the sociology of belief. It is no less and no more paradoxical than the statement that mass and bureaucratic types of organization are directly related because both depend on institutional differentiation. Indeed, mass and bureaucratic organization of urban societies is the social precondition for secularization, as we define it here.

Different belief systems with widely divergent characteristics exist side by side in urban societies, some carried by bureaucratic structures, others carried in the mass. The beliefs that help integrate an individual into his society often differ from the belief systems found within the major institutional structures of that society. As institutions become more highly differentiated, the belief systems that develop within bureaucratic structures are progressively divorced from those that are widely distributed in the population and that guide the everyday lives of individuals. In consequence, the organization of these latter beliefs is increasingly mass in type. The formal theology of the established church and the religiosity of the man in the street illustrate this. As Weber pointed out, they are unlikely to be identical (Bendix, 1960: 112-116, 143).

The structure of beliefs in an urban society is unique because of the sheer scale of organization. The individual in a peasant society belonged to a segmented, not a specialized, organization. The social structures that supported his beliefs were mostly neither mass nor bureaucratic in organization, but local or folk in character. The split between clerical and secular beliefs appeared earliest, of course, in institutions that specialized earliest, such as religion. Urban societies and the diverse beliefs they carry develop not through the growth of a single folk society but through the union of many such societies within a single organizational framework.

Consider two examples, one facetious, the other not. Take first the system of beliefs dealing with Santa Claus and the social mechanisms that perpetuate and elaborate this belief system. We learn about Santa from parents, peers, family friends, neighbors, grocery clerks, teachers in public and Sunday schools, books, magazines, radio and television programs, and department stores displays. Santa even shows up at football games, fund-raising dinners, and on street corners. Yet there are no churches, schools, corporations, research foundations, or government agencies that specially carry this belief system. Consensus on certain items such as physical appearance, number of reindeer, and residence, is high, but the belief system is not elaborate and there are other details regarding which individuals disagree. Among adult Americans, commitment can be high as long as it is protected by lack of system and/or empirical relevance. According to the present definition, this is no longer a religious belief system, a political, or even a commercial belief system. Rather, it is perpetuated by the mass organization of American society, and its characteristics reflect that organization. Hence it is a *secular* belief system.

Second, consider the personal styles of affluent persons living in the context of post-World War II bureaucratic capitalism. During the 1950s these life-styles were analyzed in a number of monographs, including Whyte's *The Organization Man*, which was concerned specifically with changing belief systems in a bureaucratizing work context, and Riesman et al.'s *The Lonely Crowd* (1950), the most salient parts of which concerned the emerging "other-directed" person and life-style. Both were concerned with a shift from what is usually called the Protestant Ethic to what Whyte (1957:7) called the Social Ethic, a belief system characterized by the three propositions that "the group is the source of creativity," "belongingness is the ultimate need of the individual," and "the application of science can achieve belongingness."

Whyte and Riesman both saw the organization ethic and other-directedness as real breaks with the past, as strikingly new belief systems generated in the process of economic (Whyte) or demographic (Riesman) change. The contrasts, inner-directedness (Riesman) and the work ethic (Whyte), are taken to represent the puritanism of earlier generations. We see *both* the work ethic and the social ethic as contemporary forms of secularized puritanism, illustrating the importance of secularization. Freed of "priesthoods and schools," beliefs are readily adapted for use in novel settings. Think of two grandsons of a white Protestant Yankee farmer. One is a used car dealer in Lorain, Ohio; the other a minor executive for Procter and Gamble in Chicago. Both meet the ghost of Cotton Mather in their dreams, but each has adapted his beliefs for use in his present life-space, one with the work ethic and the other with the social ethic.

The social ethic, though presented as a form of rebellion against its ancestor puritanism, has a remarkably similar logic in use. The essential theme of ascetic Protestantism was fulfillment of personal duty through successful effort devoted to "the calling" *in* worldly affairs (Weber, 1958).

In a sense the social ethic shows how this can be done in a corporate world. For the puritan, spontaneous emotion was evil. For the organization men and other-directed persons, strong feelings and commitments were dangerous. For the puritan, man was a tool of divine purpose; the organization man was a commodity with a value determined by a market. For the puritan, no act was irrelevant. For Whyte, organization life was a continuing series of personality tests. The themes of rejection of spontaneous or strong emotion, the commoditization of the person, and the relevance of all behavior appear to be a secularized version of puritanism unmoored from its original institutional basis in the church but still a viable and potent force in American belief. Whether the pervasiveness of analysis in terms of utility or means-ends criteria in sociology is another example of the same phenomenon is a moot but intriguing question. Several critics of contemporary sociology, specifically Gouldner (1970), have suggested something like this. To make the proposition more intriguing, there also appears to be an animus against strong feeling in some more or less contemporary social thought, for instance Fromm's *Escape From Freedom* (1941) and in a good deal of pop sociology, such as Eric Hoffer's work.[6]

As shown in child-rearing practices, beliefs appropriate to entreprenurial and bureaucratic work settings exist side by side in the same society, and even at the same level of social status in that society (Miller and Swanson, 1958). Like C. Wright Mills in *White Collar* (1956), Whyte and Riesman were right to expect the emergence of a "new middle class" with appropriate beliefs. But to expect the old middle class to disappear was merely wishful thinking. The entrepreneurs are (like the poor) always with us, and they retain their own form of secularized puritanism.

What kind of belief survives secularization: Specifically, belief systems with a strong and systematic logic that makes them

[6]See specifically Hoffer (1951).

applicable to a variety of situations by a variety of groups. Puritanism is one example, as is ju jitsu. If carried by a cult, such beliefs become strong orthodoxies, but as secularized beliefs they lend themselves especially to novel uses under new social conditions.

Secularization, it must be hastily added, does not tell the whole story of the overall structure of beliefs in American society. As discussed in more detail below, even secular belief systems are strongly conditioned by the simultaneous existence of related belief systems developed, maintained, and propagated by bureaucratic structures. First, secular beliefs are constantly being modified by developments within institutions of advanced studies and theological seminaries. The man on the street may incorporate the uncertainty principle and neoorthodoxy in his own system of beliefs on the basis of little more understanding of their meaning or intellectual context than is implied in having heard the words. Great bureaucracies serve as authorities to which one may appeal regarding "correct" (or at least fashionable) belief. Similarly, a person may feel that he needs no belief at all about some aspect of life because "the Department of Agriculture has that all worked out." Second, the very cultural prescriptions that adapt the individual to a bureaucratic environment, though developed by experiences in bureaucracies, are in large part passed on through mass organization. For example, a set of beliefs regarding the nature of careers is perpetuated through the structure of families, social classes, friendship groups, and the like, and receives some attention in the mass media. The "social ethic" that has been described as an adaptation to bureaucratic life conditions is kept alive by such mehcanisms as word of mouth, interaction in peer groups, and *Family Circle* magazine.

Secularization affects the characteristics of specialized belief systems carried by associations and general belief systems carried in the mass, as well as the ways these beliefs ere ssed. The unsystematic, undifferentiated mass of largely empirical beliefs with low or average commitment is strongly influenced by the availability of systematic, highly undifferentiated, often nonempirical beliefs within institutions. Commitment is kept low in the mass by feelings of incompetence, impotence, and dependency, and by the perceptions of rapid. unpredictable change which institutional bureaucracies engender in the individual. Where is the source of the individual's confidence when he must make decisions regarding health, politics, national defense, divorce, child rearing, business ethics, consumer purchases, or anything else? Increasingly, it is a generalized faith in the complex bureaucracies, not in religion or in any single institution.

The bureaucratic context weakens the effectiveness of secular beliefs. Secular beliefs often do not, in fact, produce the confidence in action that one might desire because of the confusion, helplessness, and doubt engendered by excessive reliance on bureaucratically organized knowledge. Dr. Spock's suggestion, so popular in the 1950s, that parents must be empowered to act by their own beliefs, medically current or not, is equally applicable today in other institutional areas. Individuals are often apologetic about their beliefs in art, music, religion, politics, national defense, and even sexual morals because of the very existence of "experts." We are caught between the excellence of our social expertise and the necessity of responsible individual action as nonexperts.

Secular beliefs are supported by two general urban norms that regularly accompany mass organization, namely relativism and individualism. By *relativism* we mean that one may be highly committed to a belief without expecting agreement from occupants of different statuses. By *individualism* we mean that not only do we explain other persons' strange beliefs by their social positions and backgrounds, but we accept this as a legitimate procedure. Traditional norms such as respect for elders are not strongly perpetuated by socialization in an urban environment, yet relativism and individualism are built into the very fiber of the urban personality. One may even understand that he is a Republican because of his station in life, expect others to be Democrats because of their social backgrounds, find this fact no reason to be shaken in his Republicanism, and feel that this is the right and proper state of affairs.

We should mention again here that it is an error to think of the secularization of belief as a process in which commitment is diminished. From a strictly religious point of view, this might be the case, but remembering the more general meaning we have used for the term, the two are unrelated. Commitment to highly secularized beliefs may be very great indeed, as much recent antiwar activity demonstrates.

Widespread consensus on the norm of individualism also protects secular beliefs. The *act of belief* is an inalienable individual right, and individuals may always keep their beliefs secret if they wish. You may be required to list your group memberships, social characteristics, activities, and intentions, but belief itself is sacred to the individual.

DIFFERENTIATION. The "causes" of the secularization of belief involve both the nature of differentiation and the norms that preserve the existing differentiated structure. The development and maintenance of a mass bureaucratic society produces a set of *general* belief systems which reflect the mass character of the social vehicle which carries them.[7]

1. Institutions and the social structures that implement them specialize (differentiate from one another) by exclusion, thus leaving residual, uninstitutionalized areas of life. One might suppose that subject matters or clusters of activities would differentiate through binary fission, that one group would specialize in A and the other in non-A, but this is usually not what happens. Often one splinter group will deal with A and one with B, while the parent group, dealing with all non-A plus non-B dies, leaving two narrower specialties and a great void. The philosophy of specialization might be stated: "Do what you can well, and leave the rest to someone else." In social life the process of differentiation leaves an increasing number of vacant residual categories. The organization of academic specialties displays this at its most extreme.

Institutionalized activities purporting to have relevance to the

[7]For a general reference to this process and to the theory of the mass society see Nisbet (1953).

"whole" man are particularly likely to be treated as residual categories, since they are particularly likely to have had specialties differentiate out of them, leaving the definition of the original category of activities as "whatever is left." Americans often treat religious and familial institutions as residual categories, with concomitant confusion as to what is, in fact, left. The usual social response to residual categories is development of a new specialty. Producers of mass culture and sociologists alike are constantly under pressure to define the "unique" (read specialized) functions of the church or the family. To be able to judge how well one is accomplishing a task, one must know what the task is. Churches, and Americans who think about churches, list a bewildering variety of tasks or functions for churches. One task that appears on many lists is help for the individual in integrating the various fractionated aspects of his existence.

Churches define the duties of the ministry more and more broadly in the attempt to fulfill this function, but secularization leaves the churches less and less able to do so. This is not because people are less religious (which they may or may not be), but because religious institutions (like others) are more specialized and bureaucratic. The task of providing an individual in a mass society with a means for guiding choices with values that balance the different, specialized aspects of his life is the last task one of the bureaucratic organizations in that society is equipped to handle. In consequence, many urbanites find that rather than integrating their lives, churches provide them with a new set of specialized roles and statuses which are more than ever walled off from the rest of their lives.

The social structures in the institutional areas that consist largely of residual categories probably have certain characteristics in common: diffuse organization, vague goals, and difficulties in evaluating performance, coupled with few technical skills.

It is in this context of the residual and uninstitutionalized areas of social life that new belief systems constantly arise—we discuss this in a little more detail below.

2. Another precondition for secularization is the erection of normative barriers between institutional areas for the purpose of

maintaining differentiation. For example, religious structures are carefully separated from political or government structures in the United States. This results not from the fact that job demands within religion and politics are too detailed to permit a joint specialty (which in fact they may be), but from a current value which states that it would be wrong to institutionalize religion and politics together. This is a "procedural" value, historically derived from an unresolved conflict between church and state and hence of central importance to the integration of American society. In consequence, we have no specialized social structures attempting to implement religious values through governmental or political means—no explicitly religious political party, for instance. Structures that come closest to this category, such as religious lobbies, are hedged about with restrictions and tread perilously close to the boundaries of legitimacy in the eyes of the population.

Barriers between institutional areas leave the individual in a mass organization, but they prevent the ultimate bureaucratization of American society, which might involve an organized hierarchical order among the institutional areas. It has yet to be demonstrated that totalitarian bureaucracy (which may be defined as a bureaucracy in which such barriers do *not* exist) is feasible as a long-term form of urban social organization, but there are many reasons to fear that it is. The most important reason for doubting its feasibility is the famous bureaucratic difficulty in coping with social change.

As areas of life are "left bare" by the specialization of institutions for either of the above reasons, the social structures that develop and perpetuate aspects of culture relevant to them tend necessarily to be mass in organizational type. The remaining social matrix consists of large numbers of very small and (taken altogether) loosely integrated units such as individuals, nuclear families, neighborhood groups, friendship cliques, transient social contacts, groups based on age and sex, and so on. If such groups formed a pervasive, stable, and systematic network of relationships, or if the same norms were being perpetuated in all groups of a like type, this would not necessarily entail mass organization. The network of primary relations remains loose, diffuse, and changing in urban societies, and the units tend to be culturally heterogeneous.

BELIEFS AND THE MASSIFIED AREAS OF LIFE IN URBAN SOCIETY. Perhaps the single proposition on which consensus is greatest in the various areas that deal with the sociology of belief can be stated very simply. *Systems of beliefs are functionally related to social systems.* That is, we recognize a striking tendency for the boundaries of belief systems and social systems to coincide. The actual nature of this connection is far from obvious. Despite the vast amount of energy expended on it, it remains both moot and an interesting research question.[8] The fact remains, however, that belief systems are, with some notable exceptions, carried by visible social vehicles that may be identified and described. The exceptions to this rule are belief and symbol systems so highly institutionalized that the entire society becomes their social vehicle: language and the categories of mind.

Sociologists tend to focus on the more established belief systems and their relatively more established social vehicles: churches and sects, parties and political movements. More interesting from the point of view of our sociology of belief, however, are the less institutionalized belief systems and the less institutionalized social vehicles that occur in the massified areas of society.

All societies are characterized by the presence of transient as well

[8]It seems unlikely that the regularity this paragraph describes is accidental. The nature of functional relationships, however, is difficult to ascertain for many reasons —and specifically because no critical test can yet be devised. We are inclined to regard the argument about the status of ideas as causes or consequences as a false argument which comes about because sociologists insist on arguing the way philosophers do. The question is not *which* is causal but what the connection over time is. We would suggest that the great debate with Weber's ghost sums to the statement that ideas and social organizations are linked through an endless causal loop over time, and that this conclusion emerges unavoidably from a reading of Weber (1958, 1963) and his critics, Tawney (1926, 1958), Yinger (1946, 1970), Demerath and Hammond (1969), and Samuelson (1957). There is philosophic, not biological, mystery in the fact that chicken born of egg lays eggs out of which chickens are born, and so on.

as enduring social groupings. Generational groups, for instance, exist in Nuer as well as in New York, and such transient groups are likely to be social vehicles for transient belief systems. In urban mass society, such transient groups and belief systems seem especially frequent and important, frequent because so many more bases exist for them, and important if for no other reason than whole industries, such as the pop music industry, can exist to exploit their needs.

There *is* organization in the "massified" or uninstitutionalized areas of urban society, and the belief systems carried by that society reflect this organization. Such areas have a loose and shifting structure of individuals, nuclear families, neighborhood groups, and so on, and aggregates that spring up when the attention of many individuals is focused on some arresting event. In this area of society, networks of oral, visual, or written communication support the special interest worlds of consumerism and leisure participation: pro football, automania, the paramilitary, and the like. In the massified areas of society, relatively transient groups become the social vehicles for equally transient belief systems, which live as long as these groups live and die when these groups die. Fad and fashion may be regarded as the belief systems carried by highly transitory social vehicles. In contemporary urban society, belief systems that purport to refer to the "whole person" typically arise in massified areas of life.

Because of the contexts in which they arise and the kinds of social vehicles which carry them, such beliefs are unpredictable, may be powerful, and are dangerous to the procedural consensus that urban society requires (Nisbet, 1958; Kornhauser, 1960). Since they arise in the residual areas of life, the magnitude of commitment they demand and/or are accorded, the scope and direction of their goals, and the nature of the tactics of the social vehicle are under virtually no formal social control, and the limits of informal social control in urban society are well known. This is one of the major themes in the mass society literature.

The belief systems currently on the wax in urban America might be aptly labeled *neosacral.* Both continuity and change can be seen in the urban American fascination with movements of instant or do-it-yourself psychiatry from Coueism through Dale Carnegie, "peace of mind" in its various avatars including Dianetics and Scientology, the Jesus movement, the occult revival, and the current fascination with ostensibly Oriental religions and their leaders. The continuity is that these systems of belief all focus on intra- and interpersonal relations—they are classic belief systems of urban people (even if those people live in communes). The change lies in an apparent shift away from at least some ratiocination to acceptance on faith alone. A new fundamentalism, with a new intolerance to serious intellectual exercise, seems to be abroad. Some exceptions can be noted, however. Yoga, if taken more seriously than a new style of clothing, requires strenuous intellectual discipline. In politics the same thing seems generally true—the intellectualism of the socialist movement and the considerable organizational insights of the "new politics" seem to have been supplanted by the "new intolerance" and the verbose dogmatism of a romantic marxism.

SUMMARY. Urbanization leads to massification and bureaucratization, differentiation, secularization, and the rise of new belief systems suited to the structure of urban society.

Societies characterized by bureaucratization in the major institutional areas of life (excluding kinship) tend to have large areas that become massified.

In urbanization, structural differentiation leads to the divorce of beliefs from the institutions that once carried them. Beliefs and belief systems that survive this process of secularization are generally those that have a strong and systematic internal logic that makes them applicable to a variety of circumstances. Secularized beliefs are protected by the typical urban norms of relativism and individualism.

Secularization of belief does not mean loss of commitment, however. Although often perceived as loss of belief, secularization involves the following four stages. First, institutionalized beliefs become narrower in scope. Second, as various institutions become more highly specialized the area of *un*institutionatized belief grows in scope. Next, the responsible decisions of people as individuals are increasingly based on uninstitutionalized belief systems. Finally, by virtue of the much more transient social vehicles which carry them, such beliefs contrast with those that dominate the society's major institutional areas.

References

Abramson, E., H. A. Cutler, R. W. Kautz, and M. Mendelson
1958 "Social Power and Commitment: A Theoretical Statement." *American Sociological Review* **23:**15-22 (Chapter 5).

Allport, C. W.
1954 *The Nature of Prejudice*. Garden City, N.J.: Doubleday & Company, Inc.

Anderson, Alan R., and Omar K. Moore
1957 "The Formal Analysis of Normative Concepts." *American Sociological Review* **22** (February): 9-17.

Anesaki, Masaharu
1930 *History of Japanese Religion with Special Reference to the Social and Moral Life of the Nation*. London: George Routledge and Sons, Ltd.

Angell, Robert Cooley

1941 *The Integration of American Society.* New York: McGraw-Hill Book Company.

Asch, Solomon

1958 "Effects of Group Pressures Upon the Modification and Distortion of Judgments." In Eleanor Maccoby, Theodore Newcomb, and Eugene Hartley (eds.). *Readings in Social Psychology.* New York: Henry Holt and Company.

Bales, Robert F.

1950 *Interaction Process Analysis.* Cambridge, Mass.: Addison-Wesley Press.

Bandura, Albert

1969 *Principles of Behavior Modification.* New York: Holt, Rinehart and Winston, Inc.

Bendix, Reinhard

1960 *Max Weber: An Intellectual Portrait.* New York: Doubleday & Company, Inc.

Benedict, Ruth

1969 *Patterns of Culture.* Boston: Houghton Mifflin Company.

Berger, Peter L., Brigette Berger, and Hansfried Kellner

1973 *The Homeless Mind: Modernization and Consciousness.* New York: Random House.

Berger, Peter L., and Thomas Luckman

1966 *The Social Construction of Reality.* Garden City, N.J.: Doubleday & Company, Inc.

Blalock, Hubert M., and Ann Blalock

1968 *Methodology in Social Research.* New York: McGraw-Hill Book Company.

Blumer, Herbert

1946 "Collective Behavior." In A. M. Lee (ed.). *Principles of Sociology.* New York: Barnes & Noble, Inc.

1962 "Society as Symbolic Interaction." In A. M. Rose (ed.). *Human Behavior and Social Processes.* Boston: Houghton Mifflin Company.

Borhek, J. T.

1965 "A Theory of Incongruent Experience." *Pacific Sociological Review* **8:**89-95.

1965 "Role Orientations and Organizational Stability." *Human Organization* **1,** 24:332-338.

Braden, Charles
1963 *Spirits in Rebellion.* Dallas: Southern Methodist University Press.
1949 *These Also Believe.* New York: The Macmillan Company.

Brinton, Crane
1965 *Anatomy of Revolution.* New York: Random House.

Brown, R.
1965 *Social Psychology.* New York: The Free Press.

Burgess, Ernest W.
1948 "The Family in a Changing Society." *American Journal of Sociology* **54** (September): 118-125.

Burridge, Kenelm
1960 *Mambu.* New York: Harper Torch Books, Harper & Row.

Cantril, Hadley
1941 *The Psychology of Social Movements.* New York: John Wiley & Sons, Inc.
1958 *The Politics of Despair.* New York: Basic Books.

Cardwell, J. D.
1971 *Social Psychology.* Philadelphia: F. A. Davis Company.

Castaneda, Carlos
1968 *The Teachings of Don Juan: A Yaqui Way of Knowledge.* Berkeley: University of California Press.

Chapin, F. Stuart
1935 "The Protestant Church in an Urban Environment." Chapter 11. *Contemporary American Institutions.* New York: Harper & Row.

Clark, Elmer T.
1949 *The Small Sects in America.* Revised edition. New York: Abingdon-Cokesbury Press.

Clark, S. D.
1948 *Church and Sect in Canada.* Toronto: University of Toronto Press.

Cohn, Norman
1961 *Pursuit of the Millenium.* Second edition. New York: Oxford University Press.

Cohn, Werner
1955 "Jehovah's Witnesses." *The American Scholar* **24** (Summer):281-299.

Coleman, James
1957 *Community Conflict.* Glencoe, Ill.: The Free Press.

Converse, Phillip E.
1964 "The Nature of Belief Systems in Mass Publics." In David Apter (ed.). *Ideology and Discontent.* New York: The Free Press.

Crossman, Richard H. S.
1949 *The God That Failed.* New York: Harper & Row.

Demerath, N. J., III, and Phillip E. Hammond
1969 *Religion in Social Context.* New York: Random House.

Dolbeare, Kenneth, and Patricia Dolbeare
1971 *American Ideologies.* Chapter 7. Chicago: Markham Publishing Company.

Dornbusch, Sanford M.
1955 "The Military Academy as an Assimilating Institution." *Social Forces* **33:**316-321.

Douglas, Mary
1970 *Natural Symbols.* New York: Random House.
1966 *Purity and Danger: An Analysis of Concepts of Pollution and Taboo.* London: Routledge & Kegan Paul, Ltd.

Durkheim, Emile
1947 *The Division of Labor in Society.* George Simpson, trans. New York: The Free Press.
1964 *The Rules of Sociological Method.* New York: The Free Press.
1965 *The Elementary Forms of the Religious Life.* New York: The Free Press.

Dynes, Russell R.
1955 "Church-Sect Typology and Socio-Economic Status." *American Sociological Review* **2:**555-560.

Eister, Alan
1950 *Drawing Room Conversion, a Sociological Account of the Oxford Group Movement.* Durham: Duke University Press.

Encyclopaedia Brittanica
1957 edition.

Festinger, Leon
1956 *When Prophecy Fails.* Minneapolis: University of Minnesota Press.

Fromm, Erich
1941 *Escape From Freedom.* Chapter 5. New York: Rinehart & Company, Inc.

Geertz, Clifford
1964 "Ideology as a Cultural System." In David E. Apter (ed.). *Ideology and Discontent.* New York: The Free Press.

Gerth, Hans H., and C. Wright Mills
1958 *From Max Weber: Essays in Sociology.* New York: Oxford University Press.

Gibbs, Jack P.
1972 *Sociological Theory Construction.* Hinsdale,Ill.: Dryden.

Gouldner, Alvin
1970 *The Coming Crisis of Western Sociology.* New York: Basic Books.

Gouldner, H. B.
1960 "Dimensions of Organizational Commitment." *Administrative Science Quarterly* **4**: 468-498.

Gusfield, Joseph R.
1955 "Social Structure and Moral Reform: A Study of the Women's Christian Temperance Union." *American Journal of Sociology* **61:**221-232.

Harris, Nigel
1968 *Beliefs in Society.* London: Watts.

Hawthorne, Harry B.
1955 *The Doukhobors of British Columbia.* Vancouver: University of British Columbia Press.

Hoffer, Eric
1951 *The True Believer.* New York: Harper.

Holton, Daniel Clarence
1938 *National Faith of Japan: A Study in Modern Shinto.* New York: E. P. Dutton & Company Inc.

Holzner, Burkhart
1968 *Reality Construction in Society.* Cambridge, Mass.: Schenkman.

Homans, George C.
1941 "Anxiety and Ritual: The Theories of Malinowski and Radcliffe-Brown." *American Anthropologist* **43:**164-172.

Janowitz, Morris
1952 *The Community Press in an Urban Setting: The Social Elements of Urbanism.* Chicago: University of Chicago Press.

Johnson, Benton
1963 "On Church and Sect." *American Sociological Review* **28:**539-549.

Kanter, Rosabeth Moss
1968 "Commitment and Social Organization: A Study of Commitment Mechanisms in Utopian Communities." *American Sociological Review* **33:**499ff.

Kenniston, Kenneth
1968 *Young Radicals: Notes on Committed Youth.* New York: Harcourt, Brace & World, Inc.

King, C. Wendell
1956 *Social Movements in the United States.* New York: Random House.

Kornhauser, William
1960 *The Politics of Mass Society.* Glencoe, Ill.: The Free Press.
1962 *Scientists in Industry: Conflict and Accommodation.* Berkeley: University of California Press.

Kuhn, Thomas S.
1970 *The Structure of Scientific Revolutions.* Chicago: University of Chicago Press.

Lanternari, Vittorio
1963 *The Religions of the Oppressed: A Study of Modern Messianic Cults.* New York: Alfred A. Knopf, Inc.

Lazersfeld, Paul F., Bernard Berelson, and Hazel Gaudet
1948 *The People's Choice.* New York: Columbia University Press.

Lenin, V. I.
1937 "What Is To Be Done?" *Selected Works.* London: Lawrence and Wishart.

Lesser, Alexander
1933 "The Cultural Significance of the Ghost Dance." *American Anthropologist* **35** (March):108-115.

Lifton, Robert Jay
1961 *Thought Reform and the Psychology of Totalism.* New York: W. W. Norton & Company.

Linton, Ralph
1936 *The Study of Man*. New York: D. Appleton-Century Company, Inc.

Lipset, S. M.
1960 *Political Man*. Garden City, N.Y.: Doubleday & Company, Inc.

Lofland, John
1966 *Doomsday Cult*. Englewood Cliffs, N.J.: Prentice-Hall.

Lowenthal, Leo, with Norbert Guterman
1949 *Prophets of Deceit, A Study of the Techniques of the American Agitator*. New York: Harper & Row.

Malinowski, Bronislaw
1948 *Magic, Science and Religion and Other Essays*. New York: The Free Press.

Manis, Jerome G., and Bernard N. Meltzer (eds.)
1972 *Symbolic Interaction: A Reader in Social Psychology*. Boston: Allyn & Bacon, Inc.

Mannheim, Karl
1936 *Ideology and Utopia*. New York: Harcourt, Brace & World, Inc.

Marx, Karl
1954 *Capital*. Moscow: Foreign Languages Publishing House.

Marx, Karl, and Friedrich Engels
1948 *The Communist Manifesto*. New York: International Publishers, Inc.

McCullogh, Helen Craig
1959 *The Taiheiki*. New York: Columbia University Press.

McFarland, H. Neill
1967 *The Rush Hour of the Gods*. New York: The Macmillan Company.

Mead, George Herbert
1962 *Mind, Self, and Society*. Chicago: University of Chicago Press.

Merton, Robert
1949 "Social Structure and Anomie." (Chapter 4). In Robert Merton. *Social Theory and Social Structure*. Glencoe, Ill.: The Free Press.

Miller, Daniel R., and Guy E. Swanson
1958 *The Changing American Parent*. New York: John Wiley & Sons, Inc.

Mills, C. Wright
1956 *White Collar.* New York: Oxford University Press.
1940 "Methodological Consequences of the Sociology of Knowledge." *American Journal of Sociology.* Vol. 6.

Moore, Omar K.
1957 "Divination—A New Perspective." *American Anthropologist* **59:**69-74.

Neibuhr, H. Richard
1957 *The Social Sources of Denominationalism.* New York: Henry Holt and Company.

Nettler, Gwynn
1970 *Explanations.* New York: McGraw-Hill Book Company.

Nisbet, Robert A.
1953 *The Quest for Community.* New York: Oxford University Press.

Ogburn, William Fielding
1950 *Social Change.* Revised edition. New York: The Viking Press, Inc.

Park, Robert
1952 "The City and Civilization." Chapter 11 in *Modern Communities.* Glencoe, Ill.: The Free Press.

Parsons, Talcott
1951 *The Social System.* Glencoe, Ill.: The Free Press.
1954 *Essays in Sociological Theory.* Glencoe, Ill.: The Free Press.
1960 "Some Comments on the Pattern of Religious Organization in the United States." In Talcott Parsons. *Structure and Process in Modern Societies.* Glencoe, Ill.: The Free Press.
1961 "Introduction to Part II." In Parsons, Shils, Naegele, and Pitts (ed.). *Theories of Society.* New York: The Free Press. Pp. 239-264.
1967 "Christianity and Modern Industrial Society." In Talcott Parsons. *Sociological Theory and Modern Society.* New York: The Free Press. Pp. 385-421.

Parsons, Talcott, and Edward A. Shills (eds.)
1951 *Toward a General Theory of Action.* Cambridge: Harvard University Press.

Polanyi, Michael
1958 *Personal Knowledge.* Chicago: University of Chicago Press.

Pope, Liston
1942 *Millhands and Preachers.* New Haven: Yale University Press.

Rabin, A.
1965 *Growing Up in the Kibbutz.* New York: Springer-Vertag New York, Inc.

Riesman, David, Reuel Denney, and Nathan Glazer
1950 *The Lonely Crowd.* New Haven: Yale University Press.

Rokeach, Milton
1960 *The Open and Closed Mind.* New York: Basic Books.
1968 *Beliefs, Attitudes and Values.* San Francisco: Jossey-Bass.

Samuelson, Kurt
1957 *Religion and Economic Action.* E. Geoffrey French, trans. Stockholm: Scandinavian University Books.

Sansom, (Sir) George Bailey
1931 *Japan: A Short Cultural History.* New York: Century Company.

Scheibe, Karl
1970 *Beliefs and Values.* New York: Holt, Rinehart and Winston, Inc.

Schwartz, Gary
1970 *Sect Ideology and Social Status.* Chicago: University of Chicago Press.

Selznick, Phillip
1960 *The Organizational Weapon.* Glencoe, Ill.: The Free Press.

Sherif, Muzafer
1958 "Group Influences Upon the Formation of Norms and Attitudes." In Eleanor Maccoby, Theodore Newcomb, and Eugene Hartley (eds.). *Readings in Social Psychology.* New York: Henry Holt and Company.

Shils, Edward
1962 "The Theory of the Mass Society." *Diogenes* **39** (Fall).

Simmel, Georg
1955 *Conflict and the Web of Group Affiliations.* Kurt H. Wolff and Reinhard Bendix, trans. Glencoe, Ill.: The Free Press.

1950 "The Metropolis and Mental Life." In Kurt H. Wolff. *The Sociology of Georg Simmel.* Glencoe, Ill.: The Free Press.

Smelser, Neil
1957 *Social Change in the Industrial Revolution.* Chicago: University of Chicago Press.
1963 *A Theory of Collective Behavior.* New York: The Free Press.

Spiro, M.
1958 *Children of the Kibbutz.* Cambridge: Harvard University Press.

Stark, Werner
1958 *The Sociology of Knowledge.* Glencoe, Ill.: The Free Press.

Stroup, Herbert H.
1945 *The Jehovah's Witnesses.* New York: Columbia University Press.

Swanson, Guy E.
1966 *The Birth of the Gods.* Ann Arbor: University of Michigan Press Paperbacks.

Tawney, Richard Henry
1926 *Religion and the Rise of Capitalism.* New York: Harcourt, Brace & World, Inc.
1958 "Introduction." In Max Weber. *The Protestant Ethic and the Spirit of Capitalism.* New York: Charles Scribner's Sons.

Taylor, Stanley
1956 *Conceptions of Institutions and the Theory of Knowledge.* New York: Bookman Associates.

Thompson, Hunter S.
1967 *Hell's Angels.* New York: Random House.

Thomsen, Harry
1963 *The New Religions of Japan.* Rutland, Vt.: Charles E. Tuttle Company.

Tiryakian, Edward A.
1972 "Toward the Sociology of Esoteric Culture." *American Journal of Sociology* **78,** 3:491-512.

Toch, Hans
1965 *The Social Psychology of Social Movements.* Indianapolis: The Bobbs-Merrill Co., Inc.

Toennies, Ferdinand
1957 *Community and Society.* Charles P. Loomis, trans. East Lansing: Michigan State University Press.

Troeltsch, Ernst
1931 *The Social Teachings of the Christian Churches.* Olive Wyon, trans. New York: The Macmillan Company.

Wach, Joachim
1944 *Sociology of Religion.* Chicago: University of Chicago Press.

Wallace, Anthony F. C.
1966 *Anthropology of Religion.* New York: Random House.

Weber, Max
1952 *Ancient Judaism.* H. Gerth and C. W. Mills, trans. New York: The Free Press.
1958 *The Protestant Ethic and the Spirit of Capitalism.* Talcott Parsons, trans. New York: Scribner.
1963 *The Sociology of Religion.* Talcott Parsons (ed.). Ephraim Fischoff, trans. Boston: Beacon Press.

Whorf, Benjamin Lee
1956 *Language, Thought and Reality.* John B. Carroll (ed.). Cambridge: The M.I.T. Press.

Whyte, William F.
1943 *Streetcorner Society.* Chicago: University of Chicago Press.

Whyte, William H.
1957 *The Organization Man.* New York: Doubleday & Company, Inc.

Wilensky, Harold
1956 *Intellectuals in Labor Unions.* Glencoe, Ill.: The Free Press.
1964 "Mass Society and Mass Culture." *American Sociological Review* **29** (April):173-197.

Willer, Judith
1971 *The Social Determination of Knowledge.* Englewood Cliffs, N.J.: Prentice-Hall.

Wirth, Louis
1938 *Louis Wirth on Cities and Social Life.* Albert J. Reiss (ed.). Chicago: University of Chicago Press.

Yinger, John Milton
1946 *Religion in the Struggle for Power.* Durham: Duke University Press.
1970 *The Scientific Study of Religion.* New York: The Macmillan Company.

Young, Michael and Peter Willmott
1957 *Family and Kinship in East London.* Baltimore: Penguin Books, Inc.

Author Index

Subject Index